A JOURNEY IN PSALMS

DESTINATION: FREEDOM

LIFE STORIES IN POETRY

Patricia Brinkman

A JOURNEY IN PSALMS
©1997 by Patricia Brinkman
Printed in the United States of America

ISBN 1-887918-11-6

Brockton Publishing Company, Inc.
1-800-968-7065

Dedication

To my husband who steadfastly walks my journey with me, and to my children, Fred, Pamela, Deborah, John, Joseph and Tricia, who always love me in spite of my crazies.

I also want to thank all those journeymen who pray for me, walk with me, cry with me, counsel me and celebrate life with me. To all these loved ones I am forever grateful.

I also want to thank God Who richly blesses me with the gift of Himself. He has sufficiently equipped me with all that I need for this journey of life. To Him be all honor and glory forever more.

Foreword

When I first met Patty Brinkman, she was a frightened little girl wrapped in a woman's body. Through the years, and amidst her tears, she has become Patricia, a woman with determination to overcome addiction, defeat and death.

Her story is symbolized by the caterpillar becoming the butterfly, from bondage in the wilderness of this world to freedom in the resurrected life of the Lord Jesus Christ.

A Journey in Psalms, written in poetic form, tells of a modern day person's struggles with life, and shows us how they can be transformed by the grace of God into triumphs of love and glory.

Mickie Winborn
Founder of Prayer Bible Studies,
Author and International speaker

Table Of Contents

Relationships

Judgments, Culture And Opinions

Education Or A Learning Experience

Prayer

Introduction

I want to publicly thank God for His mercy and kindness to me and to honor Him by sharing my life, reflections and gratitude for His guidance. I also want to thank God for my fellow journeymen whose lives have enriched mine as our walks have intersected.

My journey has consisted of many twists and turns, ups and downs. Yet, in spite of all these detours I doggedly press on to my ultimate destination, life eternal with my Lord and Savior. There have been many detours on this road of mine. There have been times of love, times of hate, times of building, times of tearing down, times of dying to self. I could not predestine these times. However, I was not helpless in any situation. There were always choices, although often I chose wrongly! God, however, always provided me with all that I needed, though many times His solutions were not what I wanted. There was joy and purpose to be found in the journey even in the midst of pain and suffering. I was stubborn much of the time, not moving until pain pushed me on. I was slow to grow, wanting the easier, softer life. "But God"— He loved me so much. He pushed me, coerced me, guided me, disciplined me causing me to grow emotionally, academically and spiritually to heights beyond my wildest dreams. He is my guide, my friend, my ever present companion, and my journey goes on. I try not to look back. Yesterday is over; today is all I have. I'll whisper a prayer and go on my way. Thank you for listening. May our journeys meet, maybe today, for coffee or tea, a time of refreshment for you and for me.

Patricia Brinkman

Cover Art: *Russian Winter,* Tpadupt, 1904

The figure of the Russian lady carrying two buckets has great meaning for me. I purchased the painting over 25 years ago because it was so indicative of my life. Frequently my husband would ask when he came home from work at night and found me frazzled, "What new problems are in your buckets?" During this time of raising children, dogs, cats and such, I often lived from one perceived crisis to another. My coping abilities were not too swift. Gradually I have learned a remarkable truth which I would like to share with you: "We need not carry our loads alone, but can share them with God, for His grace is sufficient for all our needs, buckets and all! We need to take our burdens to the Lord and leave them there. For unless the Lord buildeth the house, we labor in vain."

Chapter One

Journeying

Journeymen

Come my fellow journeymen;
Come journey back with me
To that safe dark place
Where I was first to be.

It was dark, but oh so warm,
Connected were mom and me.
I could face anything.
I felt secure; I felt so free—

Then came trauma, like I've never known.
I was pushed forward into the unknown.
My mom, she grimaced; my mom, she strained.
I was aware of her sorrow, aware of her pain—

Then came forth a cry out of me.
I saw a new world, from the old I was free.
Free I thought to sing and dance,
Unaware now of my new stance—

I grew, my brothers, heaven knows!
I was blessed with shelter, blessed with clothes.
I was blessed with friends, with family,
But, what oh what, is wrong with me—

I advanced in years; my journey went on.
I grieved my childhood. Where had it gone?
I struggled; I strained; happiness bound.
I acted so happy; I acted the clown—

There was a deep longing, for what? God only knows!
But I filled it with liquor, parties and clothes.
The longing, it lingered; the thirst went unsuppressed.
A growing awareness, the pain must be addressed.
Why, oh why, can't I numb the pain?
The rhythm of labor comes again and again—

Remembering the time many years ago
In my mother's womb, I had to let go.
Once again, I must yield to my fate,
Another journey, another date—

Surrender I did; I was set free,
Carried by a power greater than me.
Filled with His glory, sustained by His grace,
No more the struggle, I finally found base—

My journey continues, where heaven knows?
Twisting and turning, onward I go.
Walking with courage, casting out fear,
Heading for glory, my life is so dear—

Now,

Where are you going?
Where have you been?
Who is the you
That lies within—

What is your sorrow?
What is your pain?
What is your progress?
What is your gain?

Alternate Christianity

I got up this morning,
Determined once again,
To do the masters wishes,
To follow in his plan.

I started off so eager,
Filled with hope and energy,
Til I meet my first temptation,
Twas saying no to me.

"Surely this is different;
Surely God won't care
If I should slightly deviate."
It was the devils snare.

Rational and rebelliousness
Became my battle cry.
"I'll get my life together,
Not today but before I die."

I conned myself into believing
That there was an alternate plan,
Destined to satisfy the flesh,
Destined to service man.

I plunged blindly forward
Determined to go my way.
Shutting out the voice of glory,
In my illusion I chose to stay.

Sin is now in motion,
Rushing like an angry tide,
Hell bent to consume me.
Yield and I'll surely die.

Yet a voice rose up within me:
"Choose this day whom you will serve."
He loves me and he woos me.
Twas his voice I finally heard.

Running home now, swiftly moving,
Away from evil's harm.
Running home now, swiftly moving,
Into the masters arms.
Here I find my safety.
Here I hope to stay,
Til I'm forced into battle,
Again another day.

For the battle is not over.
Salvation does not come cheap.
My soul is worth the keeping.
I'm never in too deep.

Once again I yield my will.
No alternate plan for me.
To know the Truth and Him alone
Is where I choose to be.

Forward or Backward

Forward or backward,
Backward or forward,
Which way am I going?
Can you tell me please ?
From my vantage point
I just can't see.

Forward or backward,
Backward or forward,
Moving I know ,
But my direction is blurred.
I wish there was a guarantee.
I just can't see.

Forward or backward,
Backward or forward,
The indecisiveness leaves me
Dizzy and weak.
I want clear answers,
Not someday, this week.

Onward and forward,
Regressing, who knows?
No clear decisions,
Just get up and go.
Making plans, moving around,
The same old chess board,
No new movies in town.

For each step forward,
There's two steps back.
Running the race,
And missing the track.
It's all so crazy, quite absurd,
Still I press forward,
Though I still can't see.

Lend me your eyes.
Lend me your hand.
I will return them,
As quick as I can.
Surely I won't always
Be so needy, so blind.
Surely I'll learn to see
With these eyes of mine.

Forward or backward,
Who really cares!
Backward or forward,
I'm here, I'm there.
It's just a journey,
With an uncharted map.
So, let's have some fun friend.
Let's have some laughs.

We'll support each other;
Take a picnic lunch,
A first aid kit,
For when we're in a slump.
We'll travel the highway,
Up and back.
Take lots of rope.
Give lots of slack.

Backward or forward,
Forward or backward,
Taking care of each other,
Not keeping track.
For what does it matter,
If we're up or back.
It's all about growth,
And I like that!

I Know

I know that I can do it.
I know I can, I can.
I know that I can overcome.
There's no hill too steep for man.

I know that I can climb,
Even though I slip and fall.
I know that I'm a winner.
I know I've heard the call.

"Come up my child, come higher,"
Says a spirit here in me.
"Come climb up to Mt. Zion,
Where the air is light and free."

I know that I can do it.
I know I can, I will.
I have both the grace and courage,
My future to fulfill.

So, come join me now my brothers,
There's room for one and all.
Hinds feet on high places,
Protected from the fall.

I know that I've been chosen;
I have no doubt at all,
To fly with the eagles,
To answer to the call.

I have only to desire it,
To want the best for me.
I have only to begin the climb.
No toll roads, the road is free.

I have only to move forward,
Though forces tug and pull.
I know my future awaits me;
All I need is to learn the rules.

I must learn the art of climbing,
Know the weather, dangers and such.
Be cognizant of the path I walk,
Alert from dawn to dusk.

I must move swiftly forward,
Never looking back,
Facing life's pains and problems,
With a knap-sack on my back.

Must learn to be patient.
I must listen to the wind.
I must learn to remember.
There's no failure; there's only win.

Moving now with courage,
No doubt and no lack,
Knowing now and always,
I will be equipped for the task.

The height makes me giddy,
As I move towards my goal,
For to reach my Mt. Zion,
Is to be completely whole.

I will not halt or falter,
No provisions do I lack,
For my God will sustain me,
Til I reach my goal at last.

My future lies before me.
The past has come and gone.
I've grieved my lost childhood.
I've learned a brand new song.

So, come I say my brothers.
Come journey a while with me.
Come find your Mt. Zion
Where you too will be free.

Come join me in the chorus.
Come lift your voice in praise.
We're heading for the glory,
The zenith of our days.

We'll celebrate our victory
With every step we take.
For to try is to be there.
For in trying the man we make.

Our Zion has always been there.
It's majesty in our sight.
We have only to behold it
To be thrilled with great delight.

I know that I can climb it.
I know I can, I will.
I'm heading for Mt. Zion.
I've started up the hill.

I have a brand new insight,
That's set me free indeed.
I know now my Mt. Zion
Lives right here inside me...

Where Are You Going?

Where are you going?
Where have you been?
Do you want to start
All over again?

Where are you going?
Where have you been?
What do you want,
Other than sin?

Give me your attention.
Give me your hand.
I'm going to lead you,
To the promised land.

No more sorrow
No more pain
Decrease your losses;
Increase your gain.

The father awaits you
To start anew again.
So come my brothers.
Come home again.

Where are you going?
Where have you been?
And what's going to keep you
From going back again?

Where are you going?
Where have you been?
What's your hurry
To go back again?

Listen to me brothers.
My person, please excuse.
The answers not in women.
The answers not in booze.

I'll take you to my Leader.
I'll leave you there with Him,
Knowing He will heal you.
All good things come from him.

He'll fill you with his glory.
He'll fill you with his peace.
He'll grace you with salvation
Where joy will never cease.

So, come away my brothers.
Come away with me.
Come meet your savior
Who reigns eternally.

Come away my brothers.
God waits to set us free.
Come away my brothers.
Come stand along with me.

The Struggle Is Over

The struggle is over.
There's peace at last.
I've decided to live.
The dye has been cast—

For dying is living
And loss is gain.
I'm learning the rules, Lord.
I'll play your game—

No more do I gravel,
For what was-ain't.
I've let go of the reigns.
I'm becoming a saint—

Now sainthood is easy,
Once I let go.
Carried by the spirit,
I enter the flow—

Filled with His power.
Washed by His blood.
Life is much sweeter.
No, yes buts, no shoulds—

His grace is sufficient.
His love is complete.
No more powerlessness.
No more defeat—

Just yes and amen.
I can, I will.
Here at His banquet,
I get my fill—

It's here I do come,
Each day of my life,
To be captured again,
By the love of my life—

For he's ever faithful,
So here I'll remain,
Renewed by His spirit,
Again and again—

Yes, the struggle is over,
If I'll let it be.
His kingdom has come.
He lives forever in me!

Running

I'm not ready Lord,
Not ready to quit,
Groanin and moanin and having a fit.
I'm hanging on tight,
You can see,
I'm running and running,
Running from me.

What if I find me?
Oh mercy me,
I might be happy. I might be free.
It's all too frightening.
That's a fact.
I might be precious
And I can't handle that.

So, running, running,
Running I go.
Faster and faster, Oh what a show.
If the music stops
And at last I rest,
I might be happy,
Content at best.

So, help me Father
Give up the chase.
Help me seek comfort, be safe on base.
Help me to see me
Through your loving eyes.
Let me see my beauty,
Not my disguise!

A Brand New Land

Running, running no more,
I've set my sails into the storm.
I will not falter; I will not flinch
And, if it is necessary, this ship I'll ditch.

The way of success is not readily seen,
A cry, a tear, a fit, a scream.
It may take all these and maybe more,
Weight to the back, man the ores.

Whatever the cost, onward I go,
Determined, purposed, to reach my goal.
I'll not look back; It's over and gone.
To stretch for the future, is my new song.

Ahoy there, ahoy there, come aside ye mate.
I'm on a journey; I've set a date.
Come if you care too, come lend a hand.
My ship is headed away from land.

Storms, hurricanes, typhoons and calms,
It makes no difference
If you come along.
All are welcome on this voyage to success.
You have only to want to dance the new dance.

Sway to the movement; go with the wind,
Feel the power; Don't fear where you've been.
There's healing; there's glory, a brand new land.
If you care to chance it, I'll give you a hand.

The Night Is Over-Rm. 13:12

It's over. It's finished.
The past is finally or.
It's over. It's finished.
I can finally shut the door.

The grieving has been heavy,
The heaving of the breast.
But dawn has finally come,
The grieving it has past.

New horizons, new sunsets,
New days for me and you,
The past is finally buried,
A cleansing through and through.

Grace has smiled upon us,
Life instead of death.
It is a time for the living,
Blessed peace at last.

It is over. It is finished.
Tis the cooing of the dove.
It is over. It is finished.
It tis the time for Love.

If By Chance

Oh my God, it hurts so much.
Why the struggle?
Why the fuss?
Is this the reason I was born,
Just to struggle,
To cry, to mourn?

Is there more for a girl like me,
A place to laugh,
A place to be free?
Am I doomed to a life of pain,
Multiple losses,
Very few gains?

Is it something that I did wrong?
Was I displeasing?
Did you hate my song?
Tell me Jesus, where did I error?
Was it too much playing,
Not enough prayer?

I'm listening Lord, willing to change.
Show me my error;
Lift my pain.
And, if by chance, the problems not me,
I'll be ever so grateful,
If you'll just set me free!

Mountain Climbing

My body died on the mountain top.
I couldn't take the climb.
Twas time for a new beginning.
My spirit man was fine.

He rose up from the rubble
Of dead bones and withered flesh.
He stretched and flexed and breathed a sigh
For he was free at last.

No longer was he earthly bound,
No more to suffer pain,
But ready to experience
The promises of gain.

There was glory in each chosen step,
All burdens left behind.
There was glory in the spirit man.
There was glory made divine.

I walked now in His nature,
All fear and dreading past.
There were mountains to climb victorious.
There was healing here at last.

New power and new energy,
Nothing to slow me down.
As I skimmed the sides of mountains,
New wonders had I found.

It was meant that I must die,
That I may live again.
To walk in complete fulfillment
Of God's Eternal Plan.

Purpose

What is my purpose?
Why am I here?
Where am I going?
Do I really care?

Is life a joke,
A time to frolic and play,
Or is it a journey
Going from day to day?

What is my purpose?
What shall I do?
Is there some reason,
For a me and a you?

Are we just fated,
With no will of our own,
To walk through life blindly
Afraid and alone?

Is our journey aimless,
No shore in sight,
Lost in the darkness,
No anchor, no light?

What is our purpose?
If your asking me,
I think to be perfect.
I think to be free.

Free in the spirit,
Alive in the lord,
On the journey of journeys,
I say "all aboard".

The ships going homeward;
There's room for us all.
It's a voyage not for missing.
It's a heavenly call.

So, come now my brothers.
Thinkith with me.
What is our purpose
But to be eternally free.

Time To Die

When it comes my time to die
I'll neither weep, grieve nor cry,
For to this end, I've labored long.
For to this end, I've saved this song—

"Hallelujah, praise the King.
You're my glory, my everything.
To see your face, your majesty,
For this I've longed, to be free in Thee—

Free my King, forevermore,
Free to love thee and adore,
Hallelujah, Praise my King,
Forever more, to thee I'll sing.

For to praise Thee and to see Thee,
For your beauty to behold,
You're all I've ever needed.
You're the filler of my soul!

Going Home From the Hospital

Hear this, Hear this!
I make this decree.
No administer of medicine do I want to be.
Xanax, Atavan, little white pills,
Some to make you better,
Some to make you ill.

It's all in the sense of fair play.
This I know.
But a job I wouldn't want,
I just want to go.

Go home to my house
Where aspirins supreme,
Where a little headache can be fixed
By Bluebell ice cream.

I thank all the doctors,
Nurses, aids and such,
But if the truth were known,
Out of this place I'd like to bust.

The people are delightful,
The service it is great.
But I'd like the safety of my home
Eating on my own little plate.

Rise Up And Live

Rise up and live
My precious child.
Rise up and live
Before you die.

This is the moment.
This is the time,
To stand up and sing,
To make life thine.

Swing into life.
Twirl and turn.
Feel the music.
The past you can burn.

What has been
Is gone and past.
You are free
My child at last.

Reach for the gusto.
Fight for your life.
You're worth the effort.
You're worth the strife.

Rise up; rise up.
Rise up and live.
I'll make you perfect.
Now, live child, live!

No Handicaps

I had one leg—I ran the race.
I had one arm—I set my pace.
I had one mind—set to compete.
I had one heart—One heart beat.

I had one leg—It would be enough.
I had one arm—I could carry much.
I had one mind—sound and clear.
I had one heart—no need to fear.

I had one leg—I started slow.
I had one arm—to wave "let's go".
I had one mind—twas to achieve.
I had one heart—In which to grieve.

Now I grieved my losses.
I shared with you my pain.
Now I know I'm ready
To begin my race again.

I had one leg—I'll win my race.
I had one arm—no disgrace.
I had one mind—-set on my goal.
I have one heart—I am made whole.

Where Have I Been?

I don't know where I'm going.
I don't know where I've been.
I just know that I'm traveling
   The fastest that I can.

The momentum is horrendous.
I turn and swirl and spin.
I'm flung on to nowhere,
Not knowin where I've been.

It ain't no fun at all my friend,
This hurried scattered pace.
Life shouldn't always be a challenge,
Shouldn't always be a race.

It sure would be a comfort
If I was a knowin where I am.
Then maybe It'd make a little sense
Where in the hell I've been!

My Future Here Below

My Lord I heard You speaking
As clearly as a bell.
My Lord I heard You speaking.
My future You do tell.

A future filled with happiness,
A future of delight.
A future set in motion,
A future void of fright.

How can this really be Lord,
When in this world I do abide?
Can there really be a heaven,
Here before I die?

Your Spirit gently whispers,
"I've come to set you free.
Dread and fear are cast out,
From you they have to flee."

He mounts upon a white throne,
A flowing sword in His hands.
The enemy He doth scatter,
To the abyss he has been damned.

No more will the enemy
Hold sway in my life,
For the Lord has delivered me,
From a world of sin and strife.

My Lord I've heard You speaking,
Though I could hardly take it in.
To think that I have been delivered
From the bondage of sin.

You have placed my feet
Firmly upon the Rock
There to reign in glory.
All Your gifts I have got.

You, who are the Great one,
Have ordained it to be so,
That I will share Your Kingdom,
In Your kingdom here below!

Getting Healthy

Freds at the gym.
I'm on my knees.
We're both getting healthy,
The Father to please.
Care of the body and care of the soul,
Wantin to get all the wit whole.

So, listen up brothers.
Listen to me.
We need both prayer and action,
To beat disease.
God gave us both, body and mind.
To care for most diligently
or they'll crater with time!

Breaking The Bonds Of Babylon

I'm singing a song to Babylon,
As the Lord He sets me free.
I'm singing a song to Babylon,
As I head for the Red Sea.

Breaking the bonds of Babylon,
Saying my goodbyes.
No more bondage, no more shame,
Breaking all the ties.

I'm singing a song to Babylon.
Lord You did teach me well.
Fellowship with the wrong crowd,
Is neither "deebonnér" nor swell.

I learned a lot about hatred.
I learned a lot about sin.
I learned You are the only Way
And I want to begin again.

I'm moving on. My bags are packed.
I only need what's in my sack.
I've got my Lord. I've got the Rock.
I've got the power. I am good stock.

My eyes are set, goals in sight.
I know with God, I'll be alright.
No king, no chariot, no band of men,
Can thwart God's plan to leave this land.

Hallehiah! Praise the King.
Let the bells of freedom ring.
I'll dance. I'll sing. I will rejoice and pray,
Always remembering this Holy Day!

A Riddle

A riddle is a riddle,
A kind of mys-ter-y.
A riddle is no blessing,
If there is no riddler's key.

A riddle can be awful,
Full of pain and woe.
A riddle can be ugly,
If it has no place to go.

A riddle must be answered.
One must find the key
Or the riddle is no blessing,
No blessing Lord to me.

I stand at the door knocking.
Oh Lord, please here my plea.
A riddle's just a riddle
Without the riddler's key!

— Chapter Two —

Desert
Experiences

Seeking Answers

I thought and I thought,
Turned ideas upside down.
Still I do ponder,
No ideas have I found.

Shall I try this or
Shall I try that?
This questionable state,
Will drive me bats.

I need an answer.
I need a plan,
To alleviate tension,
A place to stand.

The movement is upward,
Of this I am sure.
The trumpet has sounded,
Much to endure.

In season and out,
My feet still they roam.
Maybe my answer
Is found in this poem!

ingle ells, ingle ells

Ingle ells, ingle ells,
So reads the sign.
A toast to Christmas,
No Christ divine.

Ingle ells, ingle ells,
So the song goes.
A toast to liquor,
Parties and clothes.

Ingle ells, ingle ells,
J & b scotch, drinks and thou.
No more holy season,
To drugs we do bow.

How sad, how oppressing,
This song of death.
Drinking our Christmas,
A toast to success.

We toast to our neighbor,
Our friends, family.
We play the drug game.
We call ourselves free.

It all looks so good,
Pretty bottles of wine.
Forgotten the Savior,
No King divine.

Hurrying, hurrying,
No time to think.
Into our illusion,
We do sink.

Lost in confusion,
Numbed by the booze,
Filled with the spirits,
That consume me and you.

Hear me my sisters (brothers),
Let's stop the dance.
We don't need drugs,
To have romance.

Lets' go to the Savior,
To Him let us plead.
Fill us with glory,
Please set us free.

No more ingle ells,
No more J&B.
Just the spirit of Christmas,
Alive, you and me.

So ring out the bells,
Of new freedom found.
"Away in a manger",
No longer
Drug bound.

Paper Whore

When night time comes
And no one sees,
I sneak away to my disease.
I open up the forbidden, locked door,
To gaze again on what I adore.

Excitement, yes it comes again,
As I gaze upon this female friend.
Friend, I say, though I know her not.
She's only paper but she's all I've got.

I long for something.
I know not what.
So I obsess on what I have not.
Illusion, sexual, lust and porn,
Never full and still forlorn.

What is this thing that drives me so?
I'll lose my family, this I know.
But still I press, still I fight,
To this paper whore, I have a right.

I'll risk my life, I'll risk my soul,
To caress her, my eyes to behold.
I'll drink her in, have my fill,
To return again for another thrill.

Still, in the darkness of my soul,
I long for freedom, to be whole.
Who can I tell, who can see?
I've lost myself, my dignity.

Once again, to my bed I creep,
Hoping no one knows, all will sleep.
Until again, to my stash return,
To lust again, to crave, to burn.

Many confront me, so don't you try.
I'll say I'm o.k., I'll rationalize.
I'll deny any problem, I'll curse and yell.
I'll follow this pattern straight to hell.

"It's my right, so leave me be.
If I lose all, that's up to me."
I'll sound so big, so mighty sure.
I'll fight til death, I will endure.

Back again, driven more,
In the dark of night, to the forbidden door.
The woman waits, to rape, to steal.
I surrendered my life, I've made a deal.

Now alone, my whore and me,
Twenty four hours, just she and me.
I've paid the price, for nothings free.
Gave up my wife, my family.

As I look back, it seems so absurd.
How could I lose all to a paper girl?
Yet knowing now, does not much comfort give.
I gave up all so disease could live!

Sex Rap

Syphilis, gonorrhea, herpes, aids.
Broken up families, damaged babes...

Doin what I want to, feeling fine,
Wearing blinders while others are dying...

Don't you tell me what I should do.
I'm sexually free and phooey on you...

Condoms, diaphragms, this and that,
I'll try to make it work, I'll try to make it match...

Hurrying faster, the fever runs high,
I gotta get my fix now or I might die...

Sex is king now and he's my lord.
I gotta get my fill from friend or whore...

Listen to me brother, my sisters too.
I'm talkin about me, I'm talkin about you...

It's a circular pattern, takes two to dance.
We're lookin to die, calling it romance...

People are dying, they're dying in droves.
Maybe this pattern, we'll want to close...

Save our babies, save our land;
Get healthy sexuality back in hand...

Have one partner, walk a straight life.
Enjoying the gift, without the strife...

Healthy now, my partner and me.
Living the life of m-o-n-o-g-y-n-y!

In Your Name

I did it in your name Lord.
I knew no other way.
I did it in your name Lord.
I became a human slave...

I did it in your name Lord.
Thought I had no right to live.
I did it in your name Lord.
No slack did I give...

I bound myself in misery.
I bound myself in pain.
I'd stay in my bondage.
I'd do it in your name...

No freedom, no forgiveness,
My bed I had made.
Twas the reason I existed;
For this reason I was made...

I did it in your name Lord;
For all dysfunction I'm to blame.
I did it in your name Lord.
I'll carry all the shame.

I promised to be faithful.
My vows I'll never break.
I'll continue to surrender.
Myself I will forsake...

To surrender to the wishes
Of the man that shares this home.
To give up all identity,
My very soul he owns...

He is my lord and master.
He is the king supreme.
I was born to have his babies,
To cook, to sweep, to clean...

Never mind the injustice.
Never mind the abuse.
It's not for me to wonder.
To wonder is of no use...

There is no other way Lord.
I'll have to take the blame.
If only I'd been prettier
And not so very plain...

If only I'd been wiser;
If I'd learned to tow the line.
He would'nt have to hit me.
And everything would be fine...

I hope you can forgive me Lord.
I know I made my bed.
But oh how I wish I'd chosen
To remain single instead...

The Dysfunctional Trio

SHE SAYS

"He is good;
I am bad.
He is happy;
I am sad.
He is rich;
I am poor.
He is master,
Evermore.
It is as,
It should be.
Its all about
Codependency.
He did ask;
I did chose,
For him to win,
Me too lose.
It's no one's fault,
But my own.
My own happiness,
I have blown.
So let me not criticize
This life I've chosen,
Till I die!"

HE SAYS

"She is good;
I am bad.
She is happy;
I am sad.
She is rich;
I am poor.
She is mine,
Forevermore.
Hear my pain,
My misery,
There is no chance
For a man like me.

She is power;
I am weak.
She's taken the lead,
Left her seat.
She chose to live;
I chose to die.
I can not fix her,
Though I try.
What is the answer?
How can I be free?
I's met the enemy
And it is me!"

WE SAY

"We are good,
But I am right,
And that's the reason,
Why we fight.
Determined now,
And for evermore,
To be your leader
Or hit the door.
No solution,
No compromise,
We'll keep on blaming
Until we die.
No blundery thoughts,
No hope of change,
The course's been set,
For all our days.
No concern
For you or me,
No permission,
Just to be.
A belief system
We must uphold,
Sticking only,
To what we've been
Told.
Insane, you say!
Maybe so.
But being right
Is all we know!"

53

Co-Dependency

"I hate you; don't leave me".
I hear it each day,
From codependents
Who have decided to stay.
To stay in their pain, their misery,
Determined to die,
Not to be free.

"I hate him; I shake him.
I ask him to change.
If only you loved me,
I must be to blame."
These are the words I hear them say ;
"I know it'll get better,
Maybe today".

"I owe him; I'll show him.
I can't be alone.
By friends and family, I've been disowned."
Their panic, their pain, they choose to keep.
They've pledged their troth.
They're in too deep.

Who can reach these suffering saints?
They believe in martyrdom, day after day.
They climb the scaffold to hang on a tree.
Dying daily is how they think it must be.
Misery, misery, misery me!
It's a living death this codependency.

Be Cool

Alcohol, Bourbon, Crack Cocaine,
What does it matter?
It's not in the name.

Beer, Booze, Marijuana too,
Its all a devil
That can turn on you.

Your so smug. Think your safe
Flirting with destruction.
It's no debate.

it will hook you, no matter what the name.
To destroy you,
Is the name of the game.

Play with fire, you will get burned.
Just as surely, on you,
The drugs will turn.

So listen up Brothers and don't be fooled.
Your crusin for a brusin,
The "Hard Knocks School."

Put away the bottles, the needles and such.
Come join the living.
It don't cost much.

You can do it. I know you can.
There are those that will help you,
Will lend a hand.

It's your choice. Now don't play the fool.
Come join the sane and sober.
We are where it's "cool".

The A.S.S. Word

A word so familiar, We hear it everyday,
Spoken in a most, derogatory way.

Not like spelling Mississippi, with all
Its s's and its i's.

Not a sound one likes to hear,
even if it's true.

It's coarse and harsh and most of all,
It's damage to me and you.

I pondered long, what does this mean.
Why is it so harshly used?

Why does a man so degrade himself
In the language he does use?

Today I did degrade myself.
How could I be so dumb?

I found I wasn't perfect
And I felt like I was scum.

Today I looked at you my friend
And profaned your very name

By calling you the ass
And letting you share my pain.

A.S.S, what is this word
That causes so much pain?

Where did this word originate?
Why does it carry so much shame,

A.S.S., a suffering saint
Or maybe a sinner saved?

Do you think that we could rectify
And correct this little name?

A.S.S., a sorrowful soul,
Caught in the grips of life,

Tossed and turned and struggling
And fighting for his life.

A.S.S, an animal, yes,
Chose to carry a Holy Load.

An animal blessed in a special way,
The Savior he did hold.

Do you think that it is possible,
To review this little word again,

To give it back a bit of dignity,
To move away from sin?

For it is not in the letters used,
The alphabet is fine.

It's all in what is in man's heart
That destroys or makes divine.

The Alcohol Devil

Alcohol, Alcohol, what a shame.
You took my life and left me pain.

You robbed me of my dignity.
Took my right to be free.

Left me broken, all alone.
Took my money, broke and forlorn.

Alcohol, Alcohol, You became my god.
I bowed down to your steel rod.

Curses, Curses be the day,
I took you to my home to stay.

All I had and all I owned,
You took from me and called your own.

Begging, Pleading, on my knees,
My cries of mercy you did not heed.

Such a cruel master, you did become,
Locked in your clutches of whiskey and rum.

But the fight wasn't over, had only begun,
For I found a Power, God's only Son.

Never, Never, for a life, or a day,
Will you entrap me or hold any sway.

For I have a Power that holds in His hands,
All the power that's needed to thwart your plans.

So, get on your way. Never darken my door.
You've been defeated. You lost the war.

It's, therefore, no wonder each day I do say:
"All praise to the Power Who gave length to my days."

Teen Night

A bunch of kids gather here.
They neither see nor do they hear.
Their focus is mainly on
Just getting by and getting on.

What a shame it is to me.
They miss a chance to be set free,
Free of drugs but even more,
Free to make a healthy score.

Try as we may, try as we might,
We can not force our kids to fight.
Fight for freedom, their liberty,
Their inalienable right to be free.

Still I hope, that some will choose,
To learn, to grow, to healthy move.
To these kids, I lift my hat.
"You're the winners," - keep comin back!

Rotten, Bad, Horrible

I'm Rotten, Bad Horrible;
That's Who I Am.
Destined to Die;
Accused by Man.

I'm Rotten, Bad, Horrible;
That's What They Say.
I'll Not Amount to Anything
Today or Any Day.

How Can I Be Someone
When I'm Nothing at All?
Cursed from the Day
Adam Took the Fall.

Trapped in a Body;
Not Free to Soar.
Crushed down and Broken;
A Lock on My Door.

Here I Am Father,
A Child of Thine.
Not Worthy or Able
To Get Free or Entwine.

Tangled Forever
In a Web of Deceit.
Cursed by the Devil;
I'm in Too Deep .

Turning and Twirling,
Downward I Go.
Broken and Battered,
No Place to Go.

I Turn My Thoughts Inward;
Suck in the Pain.
My Heart it Is Bursting,
With Grief and with Shame.

Running Now, Father,
In Haste I Now Move.
Running Now, Father,
Running to You.

If Your Not the Answer,
Then Fool I Will Be.
For Til Hell Freezes Over,
I Can Only Be Me.

Needyness

It Ain't Easy
Being Needy.
Always Wanting,
Never Full.
It Ain't Easy
Always Needing,
Always Feeling,
Like a Fool.

Who Can Fill Me?
Who Can Save Me?
What Can a Human like Me Do?
Am I Always
And Forever,
To Be Lost
And Confused?

Is There an Answer,
A Place of Safety,
Where Need Is Met?
Where I Will Be Full?
Onward, Onward,
Running Faster, Looking Always
But Again Marooned.

I Will Continue,
You Can Bet,
As Long as I Have Life,
As I Have Breath,
To Fill That Empty
Void Within,
To Be Satisfied,
To Conquer Sin.

I've Come A Long Way

I've come a long way Lord, from where I've been.
I've been fat and I've been thin.
I've been sober, some of the time.
I've been high—shooting a line.
I've been far and I've been close,
Seeking solutions, taking another dose.
I've been running away from me,
Just to find my life wrapped around a tree.
Try as I may, try as I might,
I just couldn't get my life right.
The journeys too long, the hills too high,
I'll just over dose and then I'll die.
The solution seems easy but my head says no.
This is no way for a man (woman) to go.
So, I went seeking answers to my hearts cry.
Who can help me if I don't want to die?
'Twas this that came from deep within:
"I'll lead you child to an eternal stream,
Where the water flows, where you'll never be dry,
Where there's power in the spirit and not the devil's lies."
So, come fellow traveler; take my hand.
I'll lead you straight to the Jesus-man.
He'll heal your spirit, satisfy your thirst,
Guide you safely; In Him you'll be emersed.
Now, try as you will, try as you can,
He'll never leave you wanting; He'll forever hold your hand.

Maybe Today

It's sad being bad,
All of the time.
It's sad being bad,
Making all life rhyme.
Rushing and running,
To that perfect place,
Where I'll lose my badness
—maybe today—

It's sad being bad;
I'm sure you'll agree.
I'd like to be you;
You'd like to me.
Hoping and praying,
That by chance,
Being someone else
Will stop the dance.
—maybe today—

It's sad being bad,
Badder than you.
For to be better,
Just wouldn't do.
I'd lose my place;
My place in hell.
Where God can't find me,
And angels won't tell—

What a dilemma!
What a pain!
I'd just like to
Breath easy.
—maybe today—

Generational Bondage

I'm afraid to love you.
I'm afraid that you might laugh
At all my fears and awkwardness
In which I have been cast—

"My Mother said—My father said",
I believed it all twas true.
My models they did lead me,
Now I bring their beliefs to you—

Who am I and can I change?
Dear, to my past I must cling.
For to find another avenue
Would only be a fling—

I must stay in the path first set,
Sad as it may seem.
For if I were to deviate,
My conscience it would scream—

What are you doing, my dear one?
Why do you hesitate?
Our family has always been this way.
Your mate must accommodate.

Now, don't you understand my dilemma,
Though it's you I truly love?
I must stay in the parameters
That are stated up above—

Control, disease, religiosity,
Call it what you may.
It's where I find my psychic.
A place that I must stay—

The Getting Even Song

(To Alanon's or Codependents)

If you want to get even,
If you've been hurt real bad,
If you want to get even,
You're angry; you're sad.
If you want to get even,
Want to ring his (her)bell,
If you want to get even,
Then friend get well!

Tend to your business.
Stretch and grow.
Tend to your business.
Learn all you can know.
Tend to your business
And I'll guarantee,
Getting even my friend,
Can be as sweet as can be.

If you want to get even,
Feel you'd like to die,
If you want to get even,
You ache inside,
If you want to get even,
Want to burn his (her) tail,
If you want to get even,
Then friend get well!

Tend to your business,
Stretch and grow.
Tend to your business,
Be made whole.
Tend to your business
And I'll guarantee,
That the God that loves you
Will set you free.

Child Of Incest

Little child, born to incest,
Little child, born to pain.
Forgive us this crime against you.
Forgive us for your shame.

You who were born of innocence,
You who were born to laugh,
We never meant such indecency,
To such a precious lad or lass.

We reach out to you, child of pain
And we ask you to forgive.
Give us child another chance
To help you to learn to live.

Mercy and forgiveness,
May not ease the pain,
But it can ease the memories
As you begin your life again.

Bogeyman

Who Oh Who is the bogeyman?
Is he a myth or is he a man?
Is he made up by me,
Just to keep me from intimacy?

Who Oh Who is the bogeyman?
Can I escape him, run as fast as I can?
Does he come when I'm asleep
To drag me down to the miry deep?

I'm here to face you bogeyman.
I can face you. I know I can.
Face to face now, no more doubt,
You have finally been found out!

Your name, I know, is False Belief,
A horrible joke—A sweet relief.
You only live in the mind of men.
You have no more power. You're no mortal man.

You came to me when I was young.
I had no way of knowing what you had done.
You stole my serenity. You stole my peace.
You left me shame based, Oh False Belief.

I'm telling you now, Oh bogeyman,
I will not tolerate your hideous hands.
Hands that steal a girls virginity,
You'll never lay another hand on me!

A Kingdom Lost

I was no king. She was no princess.
We drugged. We drank. It made no difference.
I lost my kingdom, subjects and all.
Like Humpty Dumpty, I had a great fall.

Everything dear, everything precious,
Gone forever to my drug of preference.
What can I do and what can I say?
I played the fool and now I'll pay.

The price was so high. I should have known.
But I wouldn't listen. I never went home.
Back to the bar, back to the pub,
Back to get bombed with my lady love.

So here I stand, naked and bare.
Left all alone with a drug glazed stare.
No kingdom, no power, no home, no bed,
The lady took all and left me for dead.

Do you hear me? Can you hear what I say?
Change your life or you'll be here someday.
You've seen with your eyes what drugs can do.
No fairy tale story, she'll come for you.

Run my dear brothers as fast as you can.
She'll strike like a serpent. You'll die like a lamb.
Her venom is quick, but you'll die very slow.
She wants you to suffer and she won't let go.

Build a new kingdom. Find a new land.
Fight for the right to be your own man.
No more bondage, free to be king,
Let the bells of freedom ring.

A Fairy Tale Nightmare

In the beginning, "Once Upon a Time",
It sounds so romantic. It has a nice rhyme.
Yet it comes like a robber, to steal and destroy.
It's all dressed up in pleasure, a real decoy.

A jolt of pleasure, the smell of the air,
The tilt of her head, her eyes, her hair,
Sensory pleasures, driving me on,
Locked in bondage, hushed my song.

The sound of the wind, the smell of cologne,
Blue eyes, blue jeans, in a field all alone,
One or all may be triggers for me.
I'll die to hold her; with her I feel free.

Two to three months, two to three days,
It didn't take long. I'm trapped in her gaze.
I'd die for her smell. I'd die for her sight.
I'd give you my all for a toke on the pipe.

It makes no difference what others say.
They say she's destructive. She'll leave me someday.
They say she'll destroy me. They just don't know.
She has my heart. She's captured my soul.

Sexual pleasures, orgasmic delight,
I felt so powerful, like a bird in flight.
Nothing else mattered nor did I care,
She is all that I've needed, my lady fair.

For a while I was king, high lifted up
to pleasures astounding. Cocaine filled my cup.
Paraphernalia, papers rolled up,
Bombarded with feelings, twas never enough.

Needles and pipes, cars rolling by,
For just one more hit, Lord I know I'd die.
Even the negatives, nose bleeds and such,
Held me captive; I needed a crutch.

Then came a crash like I've never known,
Paranoid feelings, depression, loss of control.
I really had lost it, shot down in flight,
Anxiety, guilt, sheer terror in the night.

No happy ending, destruction, disgrace,
The queen she'd left me for another pretty face.
She'll tease and conjure, weave her evil web.
She'll snuff out your life and leave you for dead.

Hear me my brother, will you stay by my side
As I go through my grieving, as I rationalize?
Out of control, falling now quick,
Wanting sobriety, wanting a fix.

Filled with guilt, filled with pain,
Lost my beauty, left with shame.
Lock me up. Please hold me down.
Don't let me leave or I'll go to town.

Tell me, hear me, let me talk.
I'll tell you my triggers. I'll not try to walk.
I need your assistance, your strength, your hand.
I need your courage to help me find my man.

I'll try to manipulate. I'll try to turn your head.
I'll work on your ego, focus on your life instead.
It's part of my nature, induced by the drug.
Don't accept my bull. Just give me a hug.

I know I can make it, one day at a time.
I know I can do it, given some space and time.
I know it's not all just fun and games.
I know it's a life style, sober and sane.

In the beginning, "Once Upon a Time",
There's a brand new rhythm, healthy signs.
I'm growing stronger. I'll be king of my day.
I'm living the real life. I'm sober today!

Money, Money

Money, money, shared expense,
I'm going crazy with the dance.
Does he love me? Does he not?
It's all entwined with the money he's got!
This is yours. It's not mine.
Hours spent as we dine.

Money, money, shared expense,
Sunk in bills, money drenched.
Weighted down, clothes of sweat,
The pain will come. You can bet.
Where to go, where to turn,
Real hard questions to discern.

Money, money, shared expense,
Do I want to dance the dance?
Freedom, bondage, which will it be,
Closeness, distance, for you and me?
Illusions gone, no princess be,
Turning more inside of me.

Is there courage? Is there strength?
Pressing forward, giving thanks,
Thanks for children, thanks for pain,
Thanks for labor that comes again,
Berthing now another me,
Free I pray from moneys miseries.

Money, money, shared expense,
No more dancing, no romance,
Strictly business, hard and cold,
Paying bills, being bold,
Independence, sink or swim,
No more buying on a whim.

Calculating every move,
Selling, buying, stocks improve,
Strictly business, charge or cash,
All illusion has been smashed.
Cinderela, Snow White, Rose Red,
All are fables. All are dead.
Life is real; this is true.
I'll find a way. I hope with you.

Sweet Confession

Bless me Father,
For I have sinned.
I've been to
The sweet shop again.

Once I started,
I could not stop.
I whooped down chocolate,
Hoped I wouldn't get caught.

Now it's over,
This compulsive act.
Now I'm willing
To make a pack.

I will not indulge
Til I call you first.
This guilt and shame,
It is the worst.

Faster and faster,
The candy went in.
No more caring
About this hideous sin.

So, Bless me Father,
Forgive my sin
And I'll pray your home
When I'm tempted again!

— Chapter Three —

Relationships

My Lady

Once there was a lady;
(I knew her oh so well.)
She was under an evil spirit.
Her life was a living hell.

No matter how she struggled;
(I know the story to be true.)
The spirit held her captive,
No freedom for this jew.

Her homeland was in chaos;
(I cried for her terrible plight).
Still the spirit pulled her downward
Regardless of her fight.

Twas the spirit of doubt and disbelief;
(I was afraid to even look.)
My lady she was helpless.
The dragon had her hooked.

There seemed no earthly answer;
(I had really given up.)
Then on the scene appeared a Savior,
This very evil to interrupt.

In His hand He held a sword;
(The likes I had never seen.)
It seemed to cut right to the marrow;
Ignoring evil's screams.

The woman began to grimace;
(I held my very breath).
As I saw the spirit leave her;
She began to twirl and dance.

Her family and her comrades,
(I knew her home to be Israel)
Came to celebrate her banquet.
She was free from the evil spell.

Such a happy ending;
(I never thought that it could be.)
Once evil held her tightly;
Now love had given her liberty.

I heard her joyous laughter;
(Twas music to my ears.)
She was free from all her bondage.
There was gratitude in her tears.

There was peace and blessed harmony;
(Would I tell you if it weren't true.)
There was healing beyond measure;
For my lady, God did loose.

Amen and hallelujah,
(I give all praises to the king.)
He delivered my dear lady;
To Himself He gave a queen.

To Freddy With Love

Did you ever wish
Life would go away
And you could find a place
Just to pray and play.

A place of frolic,
Free of pain.
A place of peace,
No shame or blame.
A place of comfort,
A place of glee,
A wonderful place for you and me.

We'd ride the merry-go-round,
Swing on the swings,
Praise the Father.
We'd sing and sing.
It would all be so happy,
Such gaiety,
If we could find such a place
For just you and me.

Blindman's bluff,
And kick the can,
A place for kids,
And not for man.
We'd be so happy,
Full of glee,
If we could find this place
For you and for me.

The Gingerbread Man Run

Come join the contest.
Come get your shirt.
Get a number.
Hit the dirt.
Run the distance.
Get your prize.
Your going to be eaten.
Your going to die.

It's all so silly,
Yet I know you'll join.
Your geared for disaster,
It's in your loins.
You'll run the distance.
You'll sweat and groan.
You'll give it your best.
It's all you've known.

Winning for you,
Is different, I guess.
For to be eaten
Is being the best!

Forrest Child

Rushing rivers, water falls,
All encompassing, once for all.
Flowing freely, now alive,
No more boundaries, star filled skies.

Open spaces, sheer delight,
No more cowing, no more fight.
Oceanic, great expanse,
Free to move and free to dance.

Oh what courage you have found,
To be you and not the clown.
Wearing only dignity,
Alive, awake, free to be.

Pretty lady, bathed in grace,
Forest child, chosen race.
The kingdom come is at your feet,
No more sorrow, no more defeat.

Beat the drums, fuel the fire,
Let your song rise higher and higher.
Move now freely, sway to the beat,
You're a new creature, you can't be beat.

Two Mothers

I was so blessed by You Oh Lord
By the mother you did give.
She bathed and fed and nourished me
That I may healthy live...

She gave me breath; she gave me life.
She gave me all she had,
That I may grow and flourish.
She taught me good from bad...

I thought that I had everything
But little did I know
That You were planning something more
An ever, bigger show...

A spiritual mother, who would have thought,
That I'd be blessed again.
With love and care and guidance,
You had a grander plan...

She led me to the altar,
As You dressed me as your bride.
She showered me with the Word, Oh Lord
And then she stepped aside...

My hand in Your hand, forever more,
What beauty I did behold.
My holy Mothers, they did smile.
As My God, You did make me Whole...

Daughter Of Zion

"My dear daughter, daughter of Zion,
Why do I find you crying and crying?
Don't you know you have naught to fear?
Don't you know your God is near?

Daughter of Zion, hear my plea.
It's to be close to thee.
Nothing my daughter is more important to me
But my child to be close to thee.

Your cries I hear, your moans at night.
I want you to know all is all right.
As the sparrow sings and the eagle takes flight,
So is your sweetness, so is your might.

A dichotomy I have made of thee
So you can follow close after me.
Soft and kind yet hard as nails,
A walk of victory, a walk that won't fail.

I'm leading you onward, Oh daughter of mine.
I find you precious; you are divine.
For the King of Glory has found a place in thee
And you are growing like a mighty oak tree."

Randy

Talk to me; talk to me
Before you leave.
Talk to me; talk to me.
Make me believe.

Tell me you love me.
Tell me you care.
Tell me I'll make it,
If I only dare.

Tell me there's time
And even a place
For me to abide
In this human race.

Hurry now, Hurry
Before you leave.
Hurry now, Hurry
Make me believe.

Believe in myself
As you have before.
So in power and splendor
I can grow more.

Give me a push.
Give me a shove,
Out of the nest
To new heights above.

Climbing now, soaring,
Finding new life,
In this world of wonder,
This world of strife.

Testing my wings,
Feeling the spread,
Knowing my power,
Making my bed.

It's grand; it's glorious.
I know it is true.
I find new life.
I owe it to you.

So, talk to me; talk to me
before you go.
Make me believe,
What I already know.

A Me To Us

You say we ought to be a We.
We'd like to be an Us.
But what you overlooked, my friend,
Is we are only dust.
Twill take a power greater,
Will take the hand of God,
To move these mortal bodies
Into a mode of sacrificial Love.

In love there is no competition,
No need to be the best.
In love there is surrender.
In love we could find rest.
Who knows how it did happen,
This need for being tops,
But it is into this destruction
Into this pit we did drop.

Come Oh Holy Spirit.
This is our mortal plea,
For only you can change us
From these I's into the We.
We are down and buried,
Trapped in this devilish game,
Lost and damned forever,
It tis a horrible shame.

Yet hope it remains eternal.
Our hope it lies in Thee.
Our souls they cry holy.
Come Spirit set us free.
Free to walk uprightly,
Holding each others hand,
Going about Your business,
Giving glory to Your plan.

Oh Lord, we want the We plan,
For You we surrender all.
All strongholds they must crumble,
All pride that caused the fall.
Pick us up, we pray Thee.
Set us both upon the Rock.
Heal our wounds internal.
Give us feet to walk the walk.

Point our faces in the right direction
Let all fear and accusations go.
No turning back, no hesitation,
Just a cry, "Lord here we go."
Committed to each other,
Committed to Your plan,
Our hearts in celebration,
As You recreate Your man.

Mary Glade

Mary Glade,
Mary Glade,
Child of God,
God's handmaid.

You were made special,
Uniquely knit.
A special ministry
You would fit.

Tending old
And tending young,
Running errands
Till all was done.

Always early,
Never late.
Births and funerals,
Your special dates.

Mary Glade,
We'll miss you so.
You filled our lives.
You blest our souls.

Little Dearfoot

I came to Taos, to Taos to cry.
I came to Taos and I did die.
Lost my power, lost my strength,
Surrendered my life, died in my waste.

Hear Brother Bear, Hear Sister Moon,
Here I sustained a mortal wound.
No more pride, no more song,
Release my spirit before the dawn.

I called to the Wind. I called to the Sun.
My spirit remains, the rest is dung.
For I will rise, my child and me.
We will be eternally free.

So run Little Dearfoot, run for the hills.
Live with the Elk. Hunt for the kill.
Fly with the Eagle. See with his eyes.
Find your serenity high in the skies.

Soar through the valleys. Move like the wind.
Find your peace that lies within.
No more encumbered by time and space.
Living with the spirit, each day embrace.

Here I'll live, never to die.
Living with the creatures, the Elk and I.
Free as the Eagle, no mountains to climb.
Reclaiming my power, feeling divine.

Here Little Dearfoot, you may live.
Safe to be you, free to give.
Surrounded by nature, mystery and love,
All of the gifts that come from above.

So rejoice Little Dearfoot, child of mine.
You're free to dance as your life untwines.
Sing your war chants, let the holy smoke rise,
No more mixed messages and no more lies.

You're free as the Eagle, precious as the Doe,
Watched over by the Elk, only goodness you know.
Mighty ole Elk, God and me.
Protected forever, forever free.

Gentle Fred

Gentle Fred,
God's own man.
For the truth,
He doth stand.

Storm or draught,
Feast or lean,
On God's Word,
He doth gleam.

Win or lose,
It matters not,
His steadfastness,
Is what he's got.

Onward, forward,
Pressing on,
Field and valley,
Tired and worn.

Head held high,
Body bent,
From his purpose,
He won't relent.

Working hard,
Hand to the plow,
To evil ways,
He will not bow.

Honest, truthful,
Father, Friend,
Always willing
To lend a hand.

More like Fred
Our world doth need.
Keep him safe,
Oh Lord I plead!

The Gatekeeper

There once was a gatekeeper, tall and strong.
He watcheth the castle the whole day long.
No one cometh or goeth without his say so,
For he holdeth the key; this everyone knows.

Now, it is no matter if ye be a King or a Duke,
For these important people get nary a look.
But oh, be a scullery maid,
A look from the gatekeeper could keep you away.

"What's your business? Why are you here?"
He stricketh panic in the scullery's ear.
Tis a job needed doin, she must pass through.
If she can't pass, what shall she do?

There's floors needed sweep-en, meals to be made,
Clothes to be washed and beds to be laid.
Little tasks but mighty in deed,
For these are the gifts that every king needs.

Gatekeeper, gatekeeper, heareth my plea.
The king is expecting little ole me.
Royalty passes with nary a look,
But without my services, who will cook?

Look not for credentials; I have no seal,
But what I have is important and real.
For a kingdom can't stand by a gatekeeper alone.
We all must support our King on the throne.

I Met A Man

I met a man; he blessed me.
He shared with me his pain.
I met a man; he blessed me.
I didn't even know his name.

I met a man; he blessed me.
How my heart was lifted up
As I shared with him my story
Of glory born from muck.

I, too, had walked in darkness
Not knowing where to turn
Til I met my Blessed Savior
Twas He for whom I yearned.

I, too, had tasted the bitter pill
Of hopelessness and despair
Til I met up with my Champion
Who had counted my every hair.

He told me that He loved me
And that He would never leave.
I was His forever.
I clung tight to His sleeve.

And now I walk in glory
Never more to be forlorn.
Now I walk in victory
For I have been reborn.

I met a man; He blessed me,
For he allowed me to recall,
The greatest gift to any man
Salvation for us all.

I met a man. He blessed my day.
We shared our lives, twas to pray.
We thanked Our God, where grace abounds.
We once were lost but now we're found.

Mr. Snowman

Hi Mr. Snowman,
Can you come in and play?
I have a roaring fireplace
And I'm free for the day.

My toys are very special
And there's lots for you and me.
I'd like to share my treat time.
We'll have cookies and tea.

I see you're only smiling
And I can only guess,
That you are contemplating
Being my guest.

You don't have to answer.
I want to give you time,
To think about my offer
And this date with me to dine.

It won't make no difference,
If my offer you refuse,
Cause I can come back tomorrow
And play outside with you!

Squirrels

When I went out walking,
The squirrels I did not see,
Until I felt a reign of terror
As a barrage of acorns fell on top of me.

Now, I was only passing by
No harm did I intend.
I wouldn't bother their domain,
No twig or branch would I bend.

I guess it's time we sit and talk,
For we share a common bond.
This earth was given by our God.
To each of us it does belong.

The trees are yours for fun and play,
For growing food so you won't die.
The trees are mine to build my house,
To warm me when the frost is nigh.

The trees are shelter for us both,
Protection from our dreadest foes.
You can scamper, I can climb,
So on our flesh predators won't dine.

The trees are meant to pleasure give.
I know on this you would agree.
Their beauty, height, their strength and power,
Are gift to you and me.

So, come my friend and hear me well,
There's no reason for you to fear.
I've only come to stretch my bones
Having deep regard that you live here.

Airplane Travelers

We are all together,
As we board upon this plane.
We are now just travelers,
That makes us all the same.

Seat belts on,
Trays up tight,
We are now beginning
A relationship in flight.

The plane it taxies.
We now have lift.
With our new neighbors,
Our lives we will sift.

I tell you my story,
As though you were my best friend.
I expose my secrets,
A listening ear you do lend.

A strange phenomena,
This airplane class.
Barriers fall
To a unique dance.

Bosom buddies, Confidant,
Pastor, Teacher,
We're all we've got.
So for this time, this time in space,
There is just one culture,
The Human Race.

A Trip Home

A trip home, a trip home,
Lord what can I say.
It's a close of an era,
A close of a day.

I remember the laughter.
I remember the tears.
I remember the table,
Where sharing was dear.

I remember our Father.
He sat by my side
Observing his quiver,
For us he would die.

I remember our Mother,
So loving was she.
She cradled her children
With great dignity.

I remember my siblings
All gathered around,
Fighting and fussing
And laughter abound.

We were all welcome
At this table well set.
We all knew our places.
We knew where we sat.

There hung on the wall
For all to see,
Twas our Silent Visitor,
On this we'd agree.

Our Master, Our Savior,
In Him we believed
As we prayed for His Blessings
On the food we received.

Now the laughter is silenced.
No laughter we hear.
All the people are gone,
All those we held dear.

No table, No chairs,
No smell of food.
Gone are the parents
And gone are their brood.

A trip home, such sorrow
A trip home, such pain,
Til God lays out His table,
Where we'll dine once again.

The Cry Of A Wife

Who am I?
You tell me. Who am I?

Am I a bitch,
A lazy bum,
A bit of dirt,
A bit of scum?

Who am I?
You tell me. Who am I?

Am I your wife,
Your beloved, your friend?
A person loved,
One you'd defend?

Who am I?
I ask you. Who am I?

I looked to you.
I longed to hear,
"You are my heart,
My precious dear.

You are my chosen
From years past,
To walk life through
Until we pass."

Who am I?
I ask you. Who am I?

With this in mind,
I can safely say,
My life is full.
I'm blessed today!

Scary Stuff

Scary, scary,
Scary stuff.
The sea's are rocky.
The waves are rough.
If I don't bail out
While I can, I'll surely sink,
Not to be seen again—

Scary, scary,
Scary me.
Mass confusion
Is all I see.
If there is hope,
Show me now.
I may just perish anyhow—

Scary, scary,
Scary stuff.
Just to survive,
Is not enough.
I've bailed water
As long as I can.
Now the bailing is
In your hands—

Scary, scary.
Scary you.
I don't know
What to do.
Does he care or
Does he not,
Or will he choose
This boat to rock—

Scary, scary,
Yes indeed!
Two scared people lost at sea.
Will we win or will we lose?
I'm not sure what we'll do.
But as for me,
I can say: "I will choose
To live today—

Win

Women in need.
That means me and you.
Women in need.
What can we do?

Come together,
Share our load,
For a problem shared
Is lighter to hold.

Nothing's too heavy,
No problem too great,
That we can't handle,
That we can't escape.

God say's, He'll provide,
Give us the tools,
Give light to our path,
Confound the fools.

"Come", say's the Father.
"I'll give you rest.
I'll lighten your burden.
In Me you'll be blessed."

We'll move forward,
Our backs to the plow.
We'll be successful.
We'll learn how.

We'll share. We'll study.
We'll stretch and grow.
We'll find new courage.
Our love We'll show.

We'll pull together,
No more alone.
In numbers there's strength,
Our power We'll own.

We'll push forward,
Then pull back.
There's change in movement
And that's a fact.

We're women in need
And we're proud to say:
"In needing each other,
We find Blessings today!"

I Felt

I felt put down.
I felt betrayed.
I felt embarrassed.
I felt.
I prayed.

I felt great pain.
I felt great sorrow.
I felt like there
May be no tomorrow.
I felt.
I prayed.

I felt the arrows
Going deep.
I felt the aching
In my sleep.
I felt.
I prayed.

I felt and felt.
I experienced the pain.
I felt defeated.
My spirit was drained.

I felt unloved.
I felt much blame.
I felt raw and naked.
I felt much shame.

I felt and I felt
Till I could feel no more.
I said I can't go on.
I headed for the door.

I felt separation,
Wide and deep.
I felt accusations.
I felt bittersweet.

I felt lonely.
I felt a great loss.
I felt an acute grieving
For a friendship lost.
I felt.
I prayed.

I felt perplexed.
I felt concerned.
If not to you,
Where would I turn?

I felt and felt.
What more could I do,
But to feel the experience
Of me and of you.

Maybe there's loss.
Maybe there's gain.
God only knows,
But for me it's much pain.
I felt.
I prayed.

Victorious Tiger

Once there was a tiger,
Wounded and sore was he.
He had fought a mighty battle,
With no one there to see.

His battle had been inward,
A frightening, horrible task,
Swinging at all the demons
That rose up from his past.

Now the tiger he was valiant.
His head he held high.
He really wouldn't hurt you.
He'd never hurt a fly.

And yet the animals pondered:
Why is the tiger so cast down?
What happened to his laughter?
Why does he wear a frown?

No one knew his secret,
The battle that raged inside.
No one but the tiger,
He must win or he will die.

Then came a Valiant Warrior,
All dressed and fit for war.
His amour was impregnable.
He came to settle scores.

No longer would the tiger
Have to fear and fight alone.
His anguish it was over.
He would sit upon his throne.

Now, all the jungle animals
Could not believe their ears.
The tiger purred like a kitten,
Which he hadn't done for years..

No one ever knew his secret.
It was an inside job.
From the demons he was delivered,
No more would he be robbed.

He had found a Mighty Alliance,
No more single but a team.
He'd forever walk in Victory.
It's more than he had dreamed.

No more swinging at the shadows
That loomed up in his mind.
He carries the sword of Righteousness.
He had it all the time.

Happy, happy tiger.
How happy we are for thee.
You've found an inner power
And you are forever free.

Together with your Champion,
You've taken your rightful place,
Never to be defeated,
Never more disgraced!

Little Chelsea

Little Chelsea, sweet, petite,
Quiet, gentle, not so neat.
Growing slowly, growing sure,
Watching sister, needing more.
More of mommy, more of dad,
More assurance, more of glad.
Laughing, crying,loving life.
Learning, playing, what delight!
Little Chelsea, sweet, petite,
Such a blessing, she lives on my street.

Deborah Ann, Deborah Ann

"Deborah Ann, Deborah Ann,
Child of God, Friend of man
Come my precious; take My hand.
I will guide you to your Promised Land.
I'll lead you on, lead you straight
Of this be sure; We have a date.

You've been chosen, touched by God
Not abandoned, onward trod.
The way is rocky, rough and high,
Moving upward into the sky.
Don't look down and don't look back,
Just look forward. Check your facts!

Will I leave you in your time of need?
Will I forsake my holy seed?
Did I not plant you, ask you to grow?
Have I not feed you? Child, you know.
It's I my child that presses you now,
Pressing you forward, bound to the plow.

The work's not easy; this I know.
But you are able, you'll win, you'll show.
Equipped with power from above,
Equipped to push and maybe shove,
But not for naught but for your gain,
Seeking wisdom, pressing, pushing, again, again.

Seeking Me child may cause much pain
But you will not be left lame.
Thundering hoofs, quickly you grow,
Carrying My truth as you go.
I will equip you, show you the Way,
To carry your burden, just for today."

Thirty-Third Birthday

My son your on a journey.
Now at the age of thirty-three,
Your moving towards fullfillment,
"To be free and free indeed".

Free to feel your feelings,
Free to think your thoughts,
Free to have a balance,
Between the "oughts and naughts".

Free to make decisions
Based on knowledge and wisdom both,
Free to express your person,
Free to humbly boast.

You are a child of freedom.
A child of an Immutable King.
You are a child of destiny
And for you heaven sings.

Never, never look below
But look to heaven, son, and grow.
Stand erect to your full six feet
And never give in to defeat.

Always remember to Whom you belong
And let your freedom be your song.
I thank our God for your life.
I applaud your courage, applaud your fight.

Now, I hold you in my prayers
As your seek to please God in all your affairs.
So press on my son, you're freedom bound
For when you see Him, you'll receive your crown.

Pam's Birthday

It's me oh Lord; What can I say?
It seems to be just another day.
The suns not out, a dreary day,
No sound of music, no child at play.

I know by now Lord, You have a plan.
There is a reason for where I am.
Though Your purpose alludes me, no plan do I see.
I'll continue to trust; this day is for me.

"Carry the message." These are Your words
To people less fortunate, to children of Yours.
Their lost and their weary. No road can they find.
Til their led to safety, to You Lord Divine.

I'll be the beacon. I'll be Your light,
Trusting Your promise to help with the fight.
Doors we will open, the Spirit and me.
Doors we will open so Your children can see.

Your ways are not our ways, for I'm earthly bound.
But I know your leading to a higher ground.
I'll listen intently for Your heavenly call
And watch for the crumbling of demonic walls.

You are my answer. You are my sun.
You are the reason healing has come.
So shine your light down, Oh Prince of mine,
No dreary days with my King Divine.

You brighten each day. You fill my soul.
You are the power that maketh me whole.
Lest I forget, remind me each day.
Each day is blessed when in You I stay.

Patty's Song

I do well on my feet.
I have known no defeat.
Evil had to hit the ground.
Goliath he doth fall down.

No lion or bear,
Can touch any hair,
Of the sheep that were given
Into my care.

For the Spirit of God,
In me, He doth dwell.
He gives me His power,
Against the gates of hell.

He upholds this man,
For His Holy Plan,
Tis to draw each soul
To His Jesus-Man.

Being Me

Once I felt just like me,
So airy, so light, so totally free.
My scope was broad. My sights were high.
I could do most anything. I could even fly.

Once I felt the earth was mine.
I had only to wish it and all would be fine.
I had such hopes, aspirations great,
Little did I know about my fate.

I hit the world running strong,
Light on my feet, filled with song.
I'd skip through life.
I knew I would.
Success was a given, I knew I could.

What went wrong? Where did I fall
From the pinnacle of life where I stood tall?
What could I have done to secure my dream?
Did I fail to work, to plan, to scheme?

Where is the me I used to know?
Is she lost forever? Where did she go?
If you've seen her lately, I would plead
Lead me to her, move with speed.

I'll hug her, embrace her, hold her tight,
Never again out of my sight.
I'll cherish and nurture this self of mine,
Overlook the imperfect, embrace the divine.

I've made this commitment to being me,
An awesome and heavy responsibility.
My future, my life, all in my hands,
I'll guide my thinking; I'll make my plans.

Now, life or death, it matters not
For I'll live forever thou my bones do rot.
I've made this commitment to being just me,
Today, tomorrow, Eternally—

Waiting

Here I sit waiting.
I do it all the time.
Waiting on my beloved,
His time is never mine.

Is it something about me?
Is it the way I wear my hair?
Is it something terrible, awful
Of which I'm unaware?

I'm willing to make some changes,
Meet earlier or even late.
But I'd like the assurance
That he will keep the date.

The waiters they are staring.
I know they are aware
That I am always waiting.
To let on, they would not dare!

"Can we bring you some coffee?
Is the salad to your taste?"
They try to be discrete,
Knowing I may not have a date.

It's all so confusing.
You said you'd meet me here.
I'd rather you be honest
And say "Forget our date, my dear."

I assure you I will not crumble.
My life can still be complete.
I just need an honest answer,
If you don't want to meet to eat!

Sonnet To A Turtle

Turtles aren't the cutest things.
I've never really liked them, This is true.
Yet today I create a sonnet,
Oh turtle it's to you.

I see you now dear turtle,
Like I've never seen you before,
Your courage and your fortitude,
Your calling to go forth.

Moving, slowly moving,
You never stop to dream.
You seem to have a purpose,
A goal, a call, a scheme.

Are you about the Masters work?
What is it that you hear?
What is it that keeps you going?
Do you have an inner ear?

Tis a voice that gently speaketh,
"Keep going my little one.
For you will find that which you seeketh.
For My kingdom, it has come."

What is this thing that drives you on
While carrying a heavy load?
What is this urgent quest of yours,
That doesn't let you go?

Onward, pressing onward,
As the world appears to pass you by,
And yet you do not deviate,
As to deviate would be to die.

You have an inner calling,
Not measured by time or space.
You have an inner calling.
I think I see a smile upon your face.

Happy little turtle,
Glad to be just what you are,
For you are an overcomer
As you reach out for your star.

Brand New Life

"It's a girl and we're excited."
"It's a boy and we're delighted."
It's a miracle of life,
A gift to me and to my wife.

It took time and it took pain.
It took planning. It took strain.
It took, Lord, a willing heart,
To bring forth life, A Brand New Start.

Look my friend upon this child.
Look my friend and you will smile.
Cherish now, forever more,
A Brand New Life, a girl, a boy.

Miracles we do see.
Falling stars and live oak tree,
Blooming plants from tiny seeds,
Now a brand new baby we do see.

Thanksgiving

It's early in the morning.
The dew is newly lain.
There's a certain air of mystery.
There's newness in the day.

I rise up in the darkness,
Not knowing to what I'm drawn.
But there's an excitement in my being,
As I wait upon the dawn.

Like a hunter crouched
To stalk and seek his prey,
I lay here in silence.
I lay here Lord and pray.

There is a sense of holiness,
As light begins to fill the sky.
An awareness of earths majesty
That holds both you and I.

My eyes fill with mist.
There's a pain within my chest.
Beholding all this beauty,
Fills my heart with happiness.

It's more than just a morning.
It's more than I can say.
It's the dawning of thanksgiving,
Praise God for this new day!

Dear Mommy

My dear little mommy,
You made me very glad.
You loved me and protected me
In a world that was very sad.

My dear little mommy,
You smiled and took my hand.
You led me and you guided me
Through a very troubled land.

I saw you when you were happy.
I saw you when you cried.
I saw you when you were silly.
I saw you when you died.

I saw you on your good days.
I saw you on your bad.
But I always felt secure, mommy,
No matter what a day you had.

My dear little mommy,
Let me take the time
To tell you of my love for you
Now and til the end of time.

Grieving

He cried uncontrollably.
Lord, would he every stop?
The tears came as a torrent.
Surely, there couldn't be another drop.

Sobs were seen, not just heard,
As his chest it rose and fell.
Who here could console him?
This no one could tell.

Then there came the silence,
Harder than the first.
No sign of his sorrow,
It seemed his heart would burst.

Then out of the crowd
Stepped an old man, tired and bent was he.
He reached out and embraced this brother.
Lord, I wished it had been me!

The man he heaved one more deep sigh.
I could see that he was spent.
As he fell into the arms of the stranger,
He appeared to be content.

Such sorrow, I could only guess,
That gripped that man that day,
But healing came a courting
In the dearest, strangest way.

Loss

The pain was so incredible.
I could hardly take it in.
My soul was torn, thread by thread.
It reeked my Lord of sin.

Thrashing, gnashing, an iron grip,
Torture, vengeance, no pleasant trip,
What is this thing that stabs and grabs,
Tears the flesh, thrusts and stabs?

Was I so bad to deserve this pain?
Did I not count the cost?
Was there not something redeemable,
In this relationship now lost?

The pain it is incredible.
It comes again in waves.
It lingers on for who knows how long,
For weeks, or years or days.

I give it now to you, Oh Lord.
Only You can cure Your man.
For the damage is irreparable,
For any doctor in this land.

Tricia, "Queen for a day."

Precious Tricia,
Daughter of mine.
I think you're wonderful.
I think you're fine.

I think you were sent
As a gift from above.
I'll ever be grateful
For you, for your love.

Precious Tricia,
Small, petite,
Kissed by heaven,
Love complete.

Truly blessed,
Truly kind,
Filled with purpose,
"One of a kind."

Moving forward,
Through life she goes.
The love of God
She does show.

Touching, holding,
Taking one's hand,
She'll be there for you.
She's strong as a man.

Strong in the Spirit,
Gentle as a lamb,
The wisdom of ancients
Has been placed in her hands.

Freely she gives,
Day after day,
Seeking God's purpose,
To go or to stay.

Precious Tricia,
What more can I say?
I've been blessed to know you.
Your my "Queen for a Day."

Chapter Four

Judgements, Culture and Opinions

Naturalistic Observations

Another week of observing,
It all seems very weird,
Watching people without their knowing,
Observing all their quirks and fears.

Where are they going?
Where have they been?
What is their ethnic class?
Are they fat or are they thin?

Is there a stigma surrounding their race?
Is there a reason why they hide their face?
Is there something I don't know?
Tell me now; help me to grow.

Is color an issue now?
To certain genders doth society bow?
Does one's culture fit or not,
Or are there folks that have been forgot?

All God's people, where do they fit?
Into harmony can they be knit?
But for today, all I can do,
Is observe and wonder about me and you.

Prejudice

I've watched and I've wondered.
I've pondered and observed.
What are these humans doing?
They seem so absurd.

They run; they race.
They stall; they sit.
They cry; they sigh.
They throw a fit.

One he shoves.
The other shoves back.
Some sort of contest,
It's hard to keep track.

I watch some more; I ponder more.
Just what is going on?
Some they smile; some they laugh.
Some stop and sing a song.

These humans are a funny bunch,
No accounting for their acts.
I can merely do my observing
And report to you the facts.

Peace

Peace on earth, Good will to men.
This was meant for every man.
Black and yellow, Brown and white,
About our color let's not fight.
Catholic, Protestant, saint or whore,
We all are struggling to find more.
More of life and more of peace,
Praying that suffering soon will cease.
Come my neighbor; take my hand.
Together let's find our promised land.

Discrimination

So much discrimination
I can hardly take it in.
So much discrimination
I guess I'd have to call it sin.

So much accusations
Of which one has no control.
So much finger pointing
If one does not appear whole.

Why doesn't she go on a diet?
Why can't he hold his stomach in?
Why does she wear that awful outfit?
I don't like the color of his skin.

On and on we go Lord,
Claiming to have no prejudice.
"I'm just stating facts you know,
He's too different to be one of us."

God, please have mercy.
Open up my eyes.
Let me see the truth of this,
Truth before I die.

Discord

Blacks, blacks, they do it all.
Yellows, yellows, they take the fall.
Red's, Red's. their the dredge.
White's, white's, they start the fights.

Brown's, Brown's, their the clowns.
Jew's, Jew's, their the lose.
Pray, Pray, what you say.
No one's good anyway.

Sad, sad, everyone's mad.
Blame, blame, what a shame.
Hope, hope, for no more dope.
Heal, heal, change the wheel.

Try, try, to stay alive.
Grow, grow, and just let go.
Change, change, rearrange.
This old world has gone insane.

Love, love, comes from above.
Touch, touch, it means so much.
Hold, hold, good as gold.
You, you, can be made whole.

So, Dream, dream, a brand new dream.
Walk, walk, not just talk.
Move, move, get in the grove.
Thank your God for being you.

Feel, feel, know the thrill.
Run, run, it may be fun.
Laugh, laugh, without a draft.
Sobriety, sobriety, can be a blast.

Rejoice, rejoice, you have a choice.
Sing, sing, let your bell ring.
Chose, chose, chose a friend.
He'll be with you til the end.

Democracy

Does it really matter?
Do you really care?
Is there any justice?
Can I find it anywhere?

I came here to America,
The land of the free,
Only to find oppression,
Despite the publicity.

Opportunity for one and all,
That's what I had been taught.
I trusted in my elders
And now I am so distraught.

Hate and injustice
Was in my father's land.
But America the beautiful
Promised freedom for this man.

Can we make it better
Now that we all are here?
Can we settle differences
So each of us won't fear?

I am not the enemy,
Neither sir are you.
So let us embrace each other
And freedom, let's pursue.

Bigot

I'm going to learn to be a bigot.
I'll practice every day.
I'm going to learn to hate my brother.
It may take me night and day.

I'll put in all the effort,
Of this you can be sure.
I have never been a quitter
But I've always been a doer.

Why have I chosen
To take on such a task?
It's not real clear to me, my friend,
But I'm really glad you've asked.

I see other people
Who seem to love to hate.
They seem to get a high on
Criticizing their neighbor's fate.

So, maybe I've been missing
An important part of life.
Being a real, live bigot
May be a flight from strife.

No more worrying, no more growing,
No dealing with my life,
As long as I can focus
On the screw up in your life.

Just give me someone I can criticize.
Someone I can blame,
For all the world's dysfunction,
For why the world seems so insane.

Be it color, be it race,
Be it fat people or thin,
What ever my discomfort
Is where my bigotry begins.

Now I can see the reason
Why this bigotry thing is great.
It saves me from addressing
My own, inevitable fate.

To Love, To Hate

The question is
To love   to hate.
It is a choice.
It is a debate.

I may chose to love
At the rising of the sun,
Then to hate
Til the day is done.

It is a question
To deliberate,
When to love
And when to hate?

Shall I love
When I feel good,
When life is easy
And going as it should.

Shall I hate
When pain sets in,
Failure, disappointment
And chagrin.

Scripture tells me
There's time for both.
But how to choose
I do not know.   .

So, I will go
From day to day,
To hate, to love
Which way? Which way?

I will seek
To know the truth.
I will seek
To know the time.
To love, to hate
Before I die.

132

I Have The Right

I have the right to think.
I have the right to pray.
I have the right to struggle,
With the problems of the day.

I have the right to feel.
I have the right to cry.
I have the right to care for me,
To be me before I die.

I have the right to my anger.
I have the right to feel blue.
I have the right to believe in me,
Just as much as you do.

I have the right to love.
I have the right to hate.
I have the right to know the truth,
For truth has no debate.

I have the right to righteousness,
For me the price was paid.
I have the right to be myself,
The foundation has been laid.

I have only to appropriate,
Now that I have found the key.
I have the right to celebrate,
For finally finding me!

An Ode To The Answering Machine Or That D.... Phone

If ever I get rich, I'll tell you true.
I'll destroy taped messages,
Them— not you.
First comes the message, then the beep.
The voice is business, cold not sweet.
Announcing quite clearly,
That your not home.
Leave me a message,
Speak to a phone!
The beep it rings, loud in my ear.
It's abrasive sound say's,
"I'm glad I'm not here."
It destroys my peace, my serenity.
It only brings out the beast in me.
So after each phone call,
I have to pray:
"Forgive them father;
Now, have a nice day."

Adorable, Darling, Precious

Adorable, darling, precious,
That's what men say to me,
As long as I know my place
Upon the masters knee.

Adorable, darling, precious,
Does not hold true for long,
If at man's side I try to stand
Not under him at all.

— Chapter Five —

Education or a Learning Experience

Math

Did you ever think,
Casually looking back.
You would ever study numbers.
You'd ever study math?

I can surely tell you,
And this is the gospel truth.
I thought that I would die first.
I thought that I would puke.

Now that was my yesterdays,
But those days are gone and past.
I'm working on new numbers.
I'm learning to even like math.

Miracles still happen;
To this I can testify.
Not only am I adding;
I'm working with x and y.

It's really rather thrilling
As the numbers begin to flow,
Making sounds and gestures
Like I'm really in the know.

Once again I raise my hand,
As in classes in my past.
I'm dividing and subtracting,
Making sense at last!

School

School, School
Golden Rule
Blessings now
No man's fool.

Learning, Learning
Everyday
Reading, Writing
No time to play.

Study, Study
Learning more
Taking tests
Better scores.

Lean, Lean
In to the tasks
Diligence now
No student lacks.

Write, Write
The stories blend
Into completion
When this work ends.

Glory, Glory
When the task is done
Honored by
God's own Son.

Faithful, Faithful
To the end
Now my child
The work begins.

Dear Professor

Let me tell you about the Basal Ganglia.
Oh, Listen if you please.
I studied hard and furious,
How my Ganglia could be infected with disease.

It's not the only thing I studied,
Being mindful all the while,
That you'd want to know about everything,
Cause I know that is your style.

But it seemed of grave importance,
This Basal Ganglia thing of mine
And how a disease like Huntington
Could destroy this little organ in such a short time.

For the thing I wanted to tell you
Took precedence in my thoughts,
And the things you wanted to hear about
Were frankly just forgot.

Now I know this Basal Ganglia thing
Pales in the light of day,
When I think of your test questions
And what I forgot to say.

Writing Poetry

I used to write poetry
But that was long ago.
I used to write poetry.
Somehow, I just wanted you to know.

I used to write poetry.
Twas sweet as a gentle breeze.
But now I do academics,
Creativeness had to leave.

Term papers, essays, research,
This now is the major theme,
No time for creativity,
No time for rhyme and me.

It's push on and meet deadlines.
There is no turning back.
There's a paper due by Friday,
Monday, the final task.

I used to write poetry.
It seemed important at the time.
But now my mind is captured,
Semesters control my mind.

Christmas, Easter, Birthdays,
Their meanings they did change.
They're markers just to remind me
Of the deadlines I must maintain.

Can I handle one more class?
Can my family bear the strain
As I withdraw even more
As I struggle to play the game?

I used to write poetry.
Now all of that is gone.
The scholastic life is my breath.
This world is now my song.

My only hope, my dear friend,
Is someday you'll hear me sing,
This race I have finished,
My degree my wedding ring.

A Student

I take no pleasure in school Lord;
All I feel is pain.
I take no pleasure in school Lord;
All I feel is shame.
Shame for not knowin,
What I haven't even been taught.
Shame it overwhelms me,
Leaves me lonely and distraught.

Is there not someone
Who would take me by the hand,
Lead me on to glory,
Teach me of Your plan?
Is there not someone
Who would genuionly care
If I ever learned the lessons
And if the teachings were fair?

I'm seeking now most earnestly,
Your plan to fulfill
But I surely need assistance
If I'm to do Your will.
My knees they are trembling,
My heart is surely faint.
My energies have left me.
My flesh it say's "I cant".

So come now, Lord Jesus,
From You I need a sign
That this is the mountain
That You've wanted me to climb.
I cannot keep on going,
If I do not have Your aid,
For it is a climb for experts,
Not novices or maids.

You must equip this warrior
With helmet sword and such,
Or I will surely perish
And my bones will turn to dust.
So come now, Lord Jesus,
I make my final plea.
Give me now the courage
Or Lord just set me free.

My will is always Your will.
You know my Lord tis true.
But I need Blessed Assurance
That this task has come from You.
So come my Precious Savior ,
The Savior of my soul.
Give me the tools, the willingness,
Or the courage to just fold!

Creditability

I want to be creditable.
I want to be heard when I speak.
I want to be creditable.
I want to be strong, not weak.

I want to find a place
Where I can stand secure.
I want to have a voice
That's's strong, not demure.

I want to shout the truth
Without fear or debate.
I want to say my piece.
I want to run the race.

I want to be creditable.
It's important to me
To have my credentials,
To be scholastically free,

Free to have my opinions,
Free to say what I need to say,
Free to debate with my peers,
Free to think in brand new ways,

Free to face hard issues,
Free to struggle and strain,
Using the wisdom of ancients,
Using the tools of the day.

I want to be creditable.
It's important to me.
There's freedom in knowledge.
There's creditability in a Master's degree.

Partnership Through Academics

Come let us learn together.
Let us learn to work hand in hand.
Let us climb the academic ladder,
Knowing this is all the Father's plan.

His ways are not our ways.
This has become so very clear.
Who thought after raising children
We'd find that we'd be here.

Here at the foot of education,
Ready to move and grow,
Supporting one another,
Sharing all we know.

For it is a shared effort.
Without you I would fail.
I need you close beside me
As I stretch and groan and wail.

Together there is power,
No obstacle too steep.
Our Father has set before us
A field for us to reap.

He has blessed us with each other.
He has given us the tools.
Now, He calls us to pull together,
To dump out all the rules.

No more "He should, She should"
For this is sinking sand.
No longer is this appropriate.
It's not the Father's plan.

He calls us now, "Come higher"
Unshackled from lust and pride.
He calls us into partnership,
Much work before we die.

The journey is not ending.
It has only just begun.
In helping out our brother,
God desires to make us one.

One in soul and body,
One in mind and heart,
One in the spirit,
Until death do we part.

The Test

I started out on a test of life.
I thought I was doing well
And then I faced an obsticle.
Of what matter I could not tell.

I spoke right out to it.
Pray Sir, may I pass by?
I know I've never made your acquaintance,
About this I would not lie.

He faced me with full power.
I grimaced and held my breath.
Would this be the end of me?
Would this test end in death?.

He spoke then rather gently.
I know we've never met.
But you're familiar with my children,
To them you owe a debt.

Linking, rhyming, memorizing,
Jiving words around,
Making funny images,
Turning a car into a clown,

These are a few of my family,
Journeymen along your way,
Helping and supporting,
In your brain they will stay.

"I don't intend to block you child.
Believe me, I never did.
It's just time we were introduced
If I'm to live on in your head.

I'm called by Mnemonics,
An ancient of days,
A supporter of your fellowman,
As they journeyed along this way.

My tools they are endless,
Pathways still unknown to man,
Solutions to each problem,
A blueprint for each plan.

I'll always be here for you
For I want to see you win
And if you fail in memory,
We'll just begin again.

There's no hill too steep for us.
No test we can not pass.
Mnemonically speaking,
There's a treatment for each task.

And now that we're acquainted
May I suggest you try
Another form of remembering,
Tis the Method of Loci."

High School

Back in High School
After 48 years
Nothing has changed
At least it appears.

Sitting in the office,
Waiting my turn,
Will it be praise
Or my character burned.

All the old feelings
They rise and they fall,
Memories painful
Is all I recall.

The frolic, the laughter
Was meant to defuse
The fear and the worry
When I was so confused.

Can I use thus math?
Will I understand
these global problems?
There's so many demands.

English and history
Phys Ed and Homeroom
Write me an essay
Just facts, don't presume.

Each day a new problem
My hormones they scream
I must have a boy friend
Dream some new dreams.

It's all so confusing
Neither fish nor foul.
Will I ever graduate?
Could I talk for a while.

Tell me I'll make it.
Tell me I'm O.K.
Get me some guidance.
A plan for today.

These are my memories.
These things I recall.
How I needed somebody
When there was no one at all.

Now I'm back in High school
With new hopes and plans
To assist with your schooling
The best that I can.

You'll do the work.
I'll just be an ear,
To hear and discuss
All your worst fears.

So use me, call me.
I'm back once again.
To create positive memories
Is my overall plan.

A New Intern

It's happening again.
I sit and I wait.
No plan, no decision,
No client, no date...

Reading the signs,
Observing the rules,
Saying a prayer,
Lord, what's there to do...

I'm out here in limbo,
Lost in this space.
Have no direction,
Not in the race...

Then comes to my ear,
The baa of a lamb,
Caught in the thicket
And needing a hand...

My spirits they rise.
Perhaps that's my call.
To assist my neighbor
I'm not lost at all...

Group Rap

I've got the scoop,
The scoop on the group.
It's not a place to hide.

I've got the scoop,
The latest poop.
You've gotta let go of pride.

Pride and lies,
Rollin the eyes,
Just won't get you anywhere.

You've gotta let go,
No bars hold,
For this group stuff to materialize.

It's not half bad.
You may get glad
That you were will'in to expose.

Trustin the group,
Goin threw the loop,
May help you to get whole!

Night Class

Here we are in class, Oh Lord.
The evenings dark and cold.
Each student he doth struggle,
To stay focused and controlled.

Feelings they are frayed.
The day's been extremely long.
The mind it keepeth wandering.
The body it just hangs on.

Hurry, hurry, time go by.
We're hungry and we're tired.
We must be fresh tomorrow
Or we may just get fired.

A student is only flesh and bone,
Courageous though he be.
So come sweet Jesus, release your man.
Sweet sleep is what he needs!

Statistically Speaking

Downward, downward, downward I go
Into the abyss, the abyss of the unknown.

Theory and questions, experiments and such,
So much to absorb, for this human, too much.

Downward, downward, spiralling I go,
Going to nowhere with nothing to hold.

X's and Y's, curves, deviations,
What is the standard for all of creation?

Downward, downward, abandoned my will,
Succumbed to the pressure, submit to the kill.

Flesh in submission, to die is discreet.
Moving more swiftly, there's peace in defeat.

What is the purpose? Why do I hold on?
All that I hoped for is broken and gone.

Strange ominous figures, twisted and skewed,
Pass before my vision, to be pondered and viewed.

I have no hope, now to return to my hill.
I'm plummeting downward, a weird, strange thrill.

Downward, downward, downward I go,
I'm learning my lessons, win, place or show!

Rosie, Rosie

Rosie, Rosie, What can I say?
I've gone and played the fool today.
Left my books, lost my way,
Running scared, running away.

What is the problem? What can it be?
Is going back to school thrown this fear in me?
Rosie, Rosie, lend me your ear.
I need to talk, talk about fear.

The road is long. The hills are steep.
I've made my commitment. I'm in too deep.
The bell has rung. I hurry to class.
Afraid of failure, afraid to be last.

Rosie, Rosie, just be a dear.
Hold my hand; calm my fears.
I'll do the work; plan my day.
But I need your assistance, need you to pray.

Bind the spirits that hold me down
And I'll fly like the eagle, find the high ground.
Rosie, Rosie, here we go,
Back to school to stretch and grow.

You in prayer, me in my class,
Working together, having a blast.
For learning is easy. Learning is fun.
With a friend like you, I will get done!

— Chapter Six —

Prayer

2-Corinthians 10:5

Sweet Jesus, Dear Father, Holy One of the Most High,
I entreat Thee, I love Thee, to Thee I do cry.
The road is steep, the path unmarked,
A road untraveled, bleak and stark.

Is this the direction I must take,
The way of the cross, for my Father's sake.
There's no laughter, no crying, no smiles, no tears,
Just days of nothing that blend into years.

Why such sorrow? Why such pain?
Lots of showers, just rain and more rain.
I press forward just to realize my lack,
All achievement is dung, no slap on the back.

Over and Over, I sing your song,
Jesus is Lord, come sing along.
Yet no voice do I hear, no chorus resound,
Just the sounds of silence or dollars and pounds.

Why does this money hold such sway,
Is money the King, The Truth, The Way?
Does he sit on the throne, forever in charge,
Holding the key to each mans heart.

What can man do to bring this lord down,
Raze him, destroy him, bring him aground.
Snatch his power, crush his head,
Let Jesus reign in money's stead.

I pray to you now Lord, I yield all I have,
Heal my soul with Holy Ghost salve.
Let 2-Cor. 10:5 yield a new crop,
Let strongholds fall and devilish plans flop.

Let Thy banners be flown, half mast wont do,
For You have done all that there was to do.
Let the people rejoice, the Kingdoms set free,
No fear, No anger, have power over me.

We have a new King, Righteous and Fair,
He loves intensely, He counts every hair.
He tears down strongholds with a touch of His hand,
Peace reigns forever in His Promised Land.

A Paradox

I'm here all alone lord,
With you by my side.
I think I will die lord,
Though I know it's a lie.
I find myself lonely,
Though never alone.
It's a paradox lord,
A pauper, a throne.

My crown it is tiled
Though secure it remains.
My heart it is weak.
But I'll make it today.
My life it is fragile
Yet our strong I remain,
Afraid of the enemy
Yet king of my day.

It all sounds sounds so crazy,
Hard to absorb.
I experience defeat
Yet I'm strong in the Lord.
I cry, I struggle, I fret, I moan.
I'm climbing upward
Claiming my throne.

It's hard; it's easy.
It's absurd; it's real.
It doesn't depend on how I feel.
Victory is mine.
It's been purchased for me.
I'll make it, I'll take it.
In Jesus, I'm free!

Daily Prayer

I come here each day Lord.
I come here to pray.
I come seeking wisdom,
To guide me today.

I come seeking you lord.
Your face I must see.
You are my fair leader.
Your word your decree.

I long for your comfort.
I long for your touch.
I long to be with you,
No time is enough.

You touch me; You heal me;
My very essence You see.
You guide me; You lead me,
Through tempestuous seas.

Oh what a wonder,
Your glory be.
Oh what a mystery,
You live here in me.

No wonder I come Lord.
I wish it were more.
To love and behold thee,
To praise and adore.

Your love it is endless.
Your face so divine.
To you I surrender,
For all of life's time.

I'll come seeking you lord.
I won't miss our date,
Unless I've gone homeward,
Seeing you face to face.

This time is so precious,
So filled with your grace.
A time for me only
With the King of the whole human race.

I Have A Lot To Say

I have a lot to say Lord.
I have a lot to say.
I need to know your listening,
Today and everyday.

It seems I need assurance
As I go along my way.
I need to know your there Lord
And hearing what I say.

I know I do a lot of chattering,
Some that makes no sense at all.
But I know you can cut through Lord
And heal me once for all.

I need you to do some mirroring.
I need to see your face.
I need to hear you whisper," child,
Now veer from your disgrace."

I need for Your reminder
That for me alone You came,
To free me from my guilty past,
To free me from my shame.

I need You Lord, I need you;
That's really all I have to say.
I need You Lord most earnestly,
Today and everyday.

In Your Presence

I walk in Your presence Lord,

Naked and unashamed—

I walk in Your presence Lord,

Without worry or blame—

You make me feel so whole Lord,

So totally free in me—

You make me feel so grateful Lord,

Such sweet humility—

I find Your presence awesome,

So light, such gayety—

I find You more than everything,

I find You loving me!

It Ain't Easy

It ain't easy living here Lord
But, then I guess you know.
You spent some 33 years with us
In this cesspool here below.

You brought some light and majesty
To this fallen earth of ours.
You brought some hope and healing power;
You changed some scars to stars.

You brought a song that won't be stilled;
You raised us up by Your death upon a hill;
You promised us life abundantly;
All You ask is that we follow thee.

So here we are Lord, lame and weak,
Positioned here Lord at Your feet.
Now, do the work that You do best;
Give us life and give us rest.

Lost Relationship

The pain was so incredible,
I could hardly take it in.
My soul was torn thread by thread.
It reeked my Lord of sin.

Thrashing, gnashing, an iron grip,
Torture, vengeance, no pleasant trip.
What is this thing that claws and grabs,
Tears the flesh, thrusts and stabs?

Was I so bad to deserve this pain?
Did I not count the cost?
Was there not something redeemable
In this relationship now lost?

The pain it is incredible.
It comes again in waves.
It lingers on for who knows how long,
For weeks, or years or days.

I give it now to you, Oh Lord.
Only You can cure your man.
For the damage is irreparable
For any doctor in this land.

The Day Mary Died

Glory, Glory, Glory be,
To Him Who hung upon a tree.
Glory, Glory, Glory be,
You raised me up, You set me free.

How can I ever thank Thee?
What words can I say?
Your nothing short of Wonderful.
Your the filler of my days.

You paid for all my unspoken sins.
You gave Your all to me.
Now I come before Your throne of grace
To say Oh Glory Be.

Glory to Your majesty.
Glory Great King Divine.
Glory and Thanksgivings ring
From this throat of mine.

I'll praise You and adore You.
I'll glorify Your name.
I'll give You all the glory,
Your Glories I will proclaim.

King of Kings, Savior, Lamb,
Suffering Servant, Friend of man.
Son of God, Prince of Peace,
Mighty Warrior, Love Released.

Let Me Go

Let me know or let me go,
This Oh Lord I pray.
I know You are the Truth.
I know You are the Way.

What I don't know,
Is this Oh Lord:
Is this the path that I should walk?
I don't feel very grounded
And about this I'd like to talk.

Let me know or let me go,
Tis my sincere cry today.
I want to do Your will Lord
But I'm surely afraid.

Afraid of my failures,
Afraid of my doubts,
Afraid that I won't make it,
Through the days of heat and draught.

Surely You could let me know,
Surely just a sign.
I'm not asking for a miracle,
Just a little of Your time.

So come Sweet Jesus,
And whisper in my ear.
Is this where You want me,
I'll wait right here to hear.

Be it loud or thunderous,
Be it quiet as a breeze,
I'll strain to hear Your answer,
But hurry if You please!

I Come

I come here each week lord.
I come here to pray.
I come seeking wisdom.
To guide me each day—

I come seeking you Lord.
Your face I must see.
You are my fair leader.
Your word is Your decree—

I long for Your comfort.
I long for Your touch.
I long to be with You.
No time is too much—

You teach me, You heal me.
My very essence You see.
You guide me, You lead me,
Through tempestuous season—

Oh what a wonder, Your glory be.
Oh what a mystery, You live in me.
Oh such gratitude, from me to Thee,
That You're ever faithful and present to me—

No wonder I come Lord.
I wish it were more,
To love and behold Thee,
To praise and adore—

Your love it is endless,
Your face so divine.
To You I surrender,
For all of life's time—

I'll come again next week.
I won't miss our date,
Unless I've gone homeward
Seeing You face to face—

I'll come again next week
To sit at Your feet,
To be bathed in Your glory,
To be made complete—

This time is so precious,
So filled with Your grace,
A time for me only,
With the King of the whole human race—

Who Do You Worship?

Be careful who you get on your knees to.
Child, you best beware.
For satan comes as an angel of light,
His purpose is to set a snare.

Who is it child that you worship today?
Take a really good look.
Let the spirit shine into your heart,
Every corner, crannie and nook.

For the devil he hides in many a disquise,
To you he makes it look good.
Wonder and awe, I'd die for it all,
"Come child, don't be a prude.

Everyone's doing it; it will bless mankind."
All may be traps for your soul.
For the devil intices each mans desires,
Painting a picture of man-made whole.

Be careful, my child, when you get on your knees.
You best be aware,
That the god that you worship
May just be devil's snare!

Nothing Is Too Hard For The Lord
(Based on Genesis 18:14 and Jer 32:17)

Is there anything too hard for the Lord?
I don't think so—
Is there anything He can't do?
I don't think so—
Is there anything at all, too great or too small,
Anything you know, too high or too low,
Anything too hard when your reaching for your star?
Anything at all? I don't think so—
Is there anything too hard for the Lord?
I don't think so—
Is there anything He won't do?
I don't think so—
Ask and you'll receive; He's promised this to me.
Seek and you shall find; He'll answer every time.
Knock and it will open, to the treasures you've been hopen.
For nothing is too hard for the Lord.
Amen!

Friday Prayer Meeting

Lord, I come each Friday.
I come Lord like a mouse,
To seek and search and nibble
At the Bread that's in Your house.

Here I find my substance.
It's here I'm free from strife.
It's here I find some comfort
From the problems in my life.

Here You set a table,
As though I were a king,
And make me feel important
Though I'm just a little thing.

So, I praise You for your bounty
And for those that serve the Lamb,
That I may dine each Friday
Served by my Father's hand.

Early In The Morning

It's early in the morning Lord
But not too early to pray.
Pray for help and blessings
To make it through the day.

I'm fretful and I'm restless,
Not knowing what's ahead.
I get locked into my feelings.
I get locked into my head.

I pray You help me sift through
These racing thoughts of mine
And help me find solutions
With these problems—Overtime.

I know there's no immediate fix.
The valley I must walk through.
The parting of the Red Sea,
I must leave up to You.

So lead me Lord and guide me
On this journey that I'm on.
Show me through Your Word Lord,
Safe paths to walk upon.

Draw me always to You,
Your Spirit fill my life.
With You and I together,
I'll have a better life!

Surrender

I've done about all that I can do Lord.
I know it's going to work.
I've given all to you Lord,
All my crazies and my quirks.

I tried carrying all my problems,
How silly, how insane.
Without Your grace and power,
I'm only half a brain.

I've come unto myself Lord,
Frail and broken down.
I know what I have needed
And what was needed has been found.

You are my source and power.
You are my guiding light.
You are my source of living.
You are my great delight.

Surrender is the pass word..
Into Your hands I give my man.
Heal my insides and my outsides.
Restore me according to Your plan.

Call Of The Sea

What do you want Lord?
I've heard the call of the sea.
What do you want Lord?
Just ask it of me.

Shall I walk the gauntlet
Of sorrow and pain?
Shall I feel the fury
Of the storm and the rain?

Shall I ever give in
To the call of the sea?
Nothing will I fear if
It's a call from Thee.

What do you want Lord?
Your servant asks of Thee.
Lead me by your Spirit,
All rights You have to me.

My hands are for Your bidding,
My feet to walk the plank.
My heart will do the dancing,
With praises and with thanks.

Time

There comes a time in each man's life,
A time to reflect and pray.
A time to ask, where to now?
Which way?
Which way?

There comes a time when all's not clear,
When to listen is the only call.
There comes a time when knowledge fails
And man doesn't know
At all.
At all.

There comes a time when we must move,
Not knowing where to go.
But moving now by an unknown force,
Our faith we
Must show.
Must show.

There comes a time in each man's life,
A time to yield without debate.
For to hold on, not to go on,
Is to miss
Our fate.
Our fate.

There comes at last, that final time
When time itself is gone.
The sand has passed through the hour glass.
There is the
Final gong.
The gong.

No more time to listen, no more time to pray,
No more decisions,
They were made in our yesterdays.
Now, only time eternal, a time of our choice,
A time of much sorrow or a time to rejoice.
A time of much sorrow or a time to rejoice.

Climbing Up Mt. Zion

I was climbing up Mt. Zion.
My goal to reach the top.
I was eager and attentive,
To both the heights and the drops.

My feet were firm and steady
As I began to make the climb.
My heart was ever ready.
I was going to take my time.

Then, I don't know when it happened,
The years had passed away.
I had lost most of my companions,
Laid to rest upon the way.

The distance seemed much farther
Than when I first began.
Sorrow replaced my power.
I was bent and could hardly stand.

Oh God, You know I love You.
I want to do Your will,
But this climb has lost it's fervor,
For me there is no more thrill.

My pack is soaked and heavy.
My heart is heavy la-den.
All courage it had left me,
Defeated now by Satan.

No one left behind me,
There's no-one on ahead.
The journey is so lonely,
No place to lay my head.

My nails are chipped and broken.
My hair it has turned gray.
It's really too much for me.
I want to run away.

Oh Lord, I do implore Thee.
If You can hear me now,
Answer from Your throne room,
Send out Your snow plow.

Clear away the boulders
That block me on my way.
Have mercy on Your servant.
Have mercy, Lord I pray.

Prayer For The Veterans

Here we are Lord, You and Me,
No one around, No one to see.
I press my face unto your throne,
My heart it hungers to be your own.

Come Lord Jesus, Come I say.
Show Yourself to me today.
I'm quiet now; I'm holding fast,
To feel Your presence, Here at last.

This journey Lord, with it's twist and turns,
Has me fragmented, for You I yearn.
What do I have, if not Thee?
What can I give to set these men free?

It's You, It's You, It's You and me.
Here together, here we meet.
You fill my soul; fill my life.
You give me wisdom amid the strife.

Some are lost; some can't see.
Some they search for dignity.
Some they cry; some are mute.
All afraid they'll follow suit

So much confusion, so much pain,
Feeling guilty, feeling shame.
Am I right? Am I wrong?
Weeping, wailing is their song.

Lead me Lord by Thy great light.
Show me the truth; give Your insight.
These are Your children, Yours alone.
They need Your help; they're so forlorn.

Lift their spirits; lift the drought.
Let the rains of heaven be let out.
Shower the thirsty; give new hope,
Safety in Jesus and not in their dope.

Open the flood gates; Let the rejoicing begin.
There's strength in number. Move away from sin.
Help each other. Hold a hand.
Here comes help. It's the Jesus man!

Always

I love you Lord;
(I am a mess).
I love you Lord;
(I'm in distress).

I love you Lord;
The best I can,
And then I fail,
Again , again.

How can You continue
To love me true,
When I am always
Failing You?

It seems preposterous
But this I know,
You'll love me always
Where er I go.

I love you Lord;
(I am blessed).
I love you Lord;
(You are the best).

I love you Lord;
I always will.
You gave me life;
You sustain me still.

You forgave me once.
You forgave me twice.
You gave to me,
Eternal life.

This kind of love
How can I know.
You gave me space
To stretch, to grow.

I love you Lord;
I always will.
You guide my life;
My soul you thrill.

I love you Lord;
For in spite of me
You love me always.
You set me free.

My Battle Cry

I am going to battle, Lord.
I will march on my knees.
I am going to battle.
My King I wish to please.

The banners have been raised.
My colors I have shown.
I'll march with my head held high,
For I do not fight alone.

Yahweh-Sabaoth,
He's the Leader of my team.
He holds the keys to Victory.
Of His praises do I sing.

My march is straight and steady,
No fear of turning back,
For the King has promised healing
And that takes care of that.

He yields the sword of righteousness.
He blows His mighty horn.
His angels await attentively,
From Him all life is born.

So, once again I find myself,
Bent low and bowing down,
Yielding to the King of Kings,
Knowing all evil will be bound.

Yes, I'm off to do battle.
What a privilege it will be,
To receive the spoils of Victory,
Prepared by God for me.

The World And Its Splendor

The world and all its splendor,
Was made my Lord by You.
The world and all it's splendor,
The rain, the snow, the dew.

It seemed so very easy,
Your great and glorious plan.
You had only to say the words Lord
And there were oceans, skies and land.

You set Your hand to fixin',
A very perfect land.
And then You went to makin',
A woman and a man.

Now, here I stop and ponder.
It's here I wonder why.
Up to now there was perfection.
Up to now there'd been no dying.

All the birds and creatures crawling,
They all belonged to You.
There was no disobedience.
No creature had played the fool.

There stood Your man and woman,
Clothed in glory from above.
Walking safely in the garden,
But look what Your creature does.

He turns his back on glory.
He seeks to walk alone.
He wants to have his way Lord
To erect his own throne.

The angels take to weepin.
Creatures begin to die.
Into paradise, comes corruption,
The sin of you and I.

It all seemed very hopeless.
The dye of evil had been cast.
There seemed to be no solution.
Til a Savior came at last.

There was a stirring in the earth,
A movement felt by all.
A sense of new creation,
Not experienced since the fall.

The birds began to sing again.
The trees began to clap.
The angels took to dancing.
There was joy in the earth at last.

Hallelujah, praise the Father.
He sent to us a King.
Who offered up His very life,
That we might live again.

Hallelujah, praise the Father.
The work on earth is done.
We've been restored to glory,
Through his only begotten Son.

Wisdom — Profound!

One-two-three-four-five-six-seven,
I used to think I'd go to heaven.
Seven-six-five-four-three-two-one,
I'll never make it for what I've done.
One and two and three and four,
Grace is what I'm hopin' for.
Four and three and two and one
If Jesus don't save me, I am done!

Perfect Street

I want to live on perfect street,
Where all is calm, all is neat.
I want to live forever on a street of no repair,
Where people love each other and never have a care.

I want to live abundantly,
Each day of my life,
Having no more worries,
Having no more strife.

I want it all so perfect,
No dust, no trash, no pain.
I want to spend life dancing,
Listening to each refrain.

Now, doesn't that sound like heaven,
A street with no pain or care?
Wouldn't you like to find this street
And move yourself to there?

I've been searching,
You can bet,
For a home that's perfect,
Where I will no more fret.

For I've been up and I've been down,
Every street in every town.
Asking, seeking, but to no avail.
I can't find the house, I lost the trail.

Have you seen my perfect street,
Where evils conquered, no defeat?
If you can help me, this I pray,
That you'll show me quickly,
The door, the way.

Christmas In The Woods

Down in the woods, Lord,
In the quiet of the trees,
Lays a little baby waiting,
To embrace both You and me.

His demeanor is so gentle.
His eyes they glow like fire.
To bless us with His presence,
This is His desire

His presence is so awesome.
We can hardly take it in.
Though no words are ever spoken,
There's joy just to be with Him.

Oh Precious Child of Heaven,
Oh Holy, Holy night,
Here in this darkened forest,
Is the Savior born of Light.

The wind, it whispers love songs,
As it gently blows among the trees.
The mountains cry Hosanna,
How can we ever leave.

Yet the Child says "Go now,
And arouse the sleeping land.
Tell them that the Savior cometh,
That His Kingdom is at hand.

Go and spread the Good News,
Of what you have discovered here,
That the Sleepy Babe of Heaven,
To His children has appeared."

My Religion

I have a working religion.
I know this as a fact.
For my religion is based on the man Jesus,
That's all there is to that—

The formula is very simple.
The rules are very clear.
I need only to cleave to my Master,
The one I hold so dear—

He guides my very footsteps.
He lifts me when I fall.
He gives me clear directions.
It's really not hard at all—

Each day I check the road map.
The one He did provide.
If I follow His instructions,
I know I'll never die—

I will live on forever,
In the bosom of the Lamb.
I will live on eternally.
My hope is in the Man—

This man was sent by God,
His precious only Son.
My hope is based on this relationship,
For in Him all the work was done—

I hope that you can see now
Why my religion works.
It's based solely on the person
Who made the universe—

No Early Bird

It's early in the morning,
Early Lord for me,
For I'm not an early riser,
Lord You know it's me.

Others have already been here
To listen to their King.
Others have already received their blessing,
Gave praises as they sing.

None the less I come Sir,
Moving by my time clock.
It may be rather faulty
But it's the only one I've got.

I want to be Your servant.
I want to do Your will.
I want to bask in Your presence
I want to get my fill.

I know You don't serve left overs
No matter when I came.
You set out Your bounty.
You always are the same

It's more than I can imagine.
Your such a gracious Host.
There's nothing ever lacking,
I lift my glass to toast.

I'll toast You, my dear Father
For all Your faithfulness.
I lift my heart to praise Thee.
For here I'm always blest.

I'll try to be more prompt, Sir,
Try to get here on time,
Knowing You'll be waiting
To fill me with more rhymes.

I love our time together.
I love all Your gifts.
But I love You most of all
For Your loving tenderness!

Down In The Valley

In the peace of Your presence,
I do find rest.
In the peace of Your presence,
I do my best.
It's here in your presence,
Alone at your feet
That I fill my cup, as our spirits meet,
You on Your throne,
Me by Your side,
Secure in your presence,
You as my guide,

No one to harm me, pain far away,
Equipped with Your mercy,
Wanting to stay.
Yet I hear Your voice:
"Move on my child.
I'll never leave you.
I'll always be your guide."
Yet into the valley
You must go,
To stretch, to prosper,
To learn, to grow.

It's there in the valley
That the schooling is done.
It's there in the valley
My Will will be done.
So fear not my child
As you leave this place.
You'll return tomorrow
For more love, more grace.
In the peace of My presence
You'll once again find
A days provision
On which you will dine.

I'll fill you with love,
Mercy and grace.
I'll fill your basket;
I'll kiss your face.
I'll lead you onward,
To greater heights.
For it is in the valleys
That you'll fight the good fights.
I will lead you forward.
I'll instruct you well.
My power and my glory
In your heart will swell.

"Peace with you"
You'll hear Me say.
Daddy Loves you
And He's here to stay.
So be encouraged
As you face another day.
The battle is won,
The devil kept at bay.
It's time to get excited,
Hold your head up high,
Tis the King of Glory
Who resides at your side.

The Christmas Eve Song

The Lord always comes
When man is not ready.
The Lord always comes in the still of the night.
The Lord always comes when man's hearts are yearning.
The Lord always comes,
The Lord always comes,
The Lord always comes,
At just the right time.

The Lord always comes
When the whole world is sleeping.
The Lord always comes to bring forth new light.
The Lord always comes to His precious children.
The Lord always comes,
The Lord always comes,
The Lord always comes,
At just the right time!

The Lord always comes
With love and forgiveness .
The Lord always comes when there's no hope in sight.
The Lord always comes to bless His dear children.
The Lord always comes,
The Lord always comes,
The Lord always comes,
He's coming tonight!

Wisdom and Discretion

Wisdom and discretion were with God
When He created the World.
Wisdom and discretion are with me now
As His glorious truths are unfurled.
Yes I really know it, of this there is no doubt.
Jesus has chosen me to put the fires of doubt out.

Doubting is for sinners, not for kingdom kids.
Doubting has no place now, of doubt's powers I've been rid.
Jesus has made a way where I can walk and sing,
Where joy is unbounded and the bells of freedom ring.
Is there any doubt then of the mercy of God's Man
Who came into this unworthy world, as a sacrificial Lamb?

Glory and Hallelujah tis in the heart of this man
For the Savior has redeemed me and given me the land.
Yes, is it any wonder, that I cast old doubt out?
For he has been defeated it was a worthy bout.
I stood upon the Rock; I firmly took a stand
And the army of the Living God became my right hand.

God thrust a mighty lightening bolt that streaked across the sky.
And doubt and fear, they fell at last. God's power they could not deny.
Doubt and fear they fell defeated now. No more could they return.
For their devilish game was thwarted. In hell's fire they'd have to burn.
I breathed a sigh and took my place with the ancients of the past
Knowing God had set me free. In His presence I do bask.

A Mission

Hear the Spirit calling:
"My kingdom is at hand".
Twill be my only message,
As I travel through the land

I've been given a mission.
Within my allotted time
And I want each hour to count Lord,
As I make my final climb.

Empowered by Your Spirit,
Face pointed into the wind.
These hours and days are precious
As souls I hope to win.

"Come and be satisfied
Come and be set Free".
The Spirit He is calling.
He's calling you through me.

Come and sit and talk awhile.
We'll find the strength we need,
To conquer principalities
And set the captives free.

It's the now that is important, child
Tomorrow may never be.
The now is a Holy hour,
As the spirit calls to thee.

So lift your eyes to heaven
Dry the tears from your eyes.
Today the King He cometh.
Today He will arrive.

No fear for tomorrow.
Oh death he has no sting.
For every hour and every moment
Is blessed in service to the King!

Cradle Me Jesus

Hold me, precious Jesus.
Cradle me in your arms.
Hold me, precious Jesus.
Keep me from life's harms.

Hold me, precious Jesus,
Til time has past away.
And You and I live together,
Til the Zenith of the days.

Tis all I've ever longed for,
To be held in Your arms.
Tis all I've ever wanted,
To be guiled by Your charms.

Tis all I've ever needed.
This I've come to know.
Your are the Alpha and Omega,
The fulfillment of my soul.

Hold me, precious Jesus,
Cradle me real tight.
Til there is no more struggle.
Til I have ceased to fight.

Hold me, precious Jesus,
Err my feet go astray.
Hold me, precious Jesus,
Today and everyday.

A Miracle

Today I will remember.
Today I won't forget,
That I'm part of a miracle.
God's not finished with me yet.

I can move with much assurance.
I can do my very best,
But I can't add to the miracle,
For God must do all the rest.

I can make decisions.
I can mold and shape a plan.
I can formulate life goals.
I can try to be a man.

I can learn and study science.
I can hold a dying hand.
I can listen to a bird sing.
I can direct and lead a band.

I can make many things.
I can live and I can die,
But I can't make a miracle,
No matter how I try!

On My Knees

It's been a long time Lord,
School, classes, sickness and disease,
A falling away from being here on my knees.
Hear my cry Lord. Help me now to bow.
For I'm filled with your Spirit. Lord I know how.

It's doing the doing, taking the time,
Seeking Your face, making a rhyme.
It's here I find joy, wisdom and such.
It's here my heart pounds. You are so much.

Hold me now Jesus as my flesh wants to run.
Settle my spirit. Join us as one.
You are my strength, my power, my friend.
It's You that gives courage. Your gospel I defend.

Come quickly Lord Jesus. Give me a song.
Give me a sign that I can lean on.
Holding me now tightly. Don't let me go.
You are
my glory. You filleth my soul.

"My journey has not been an isolated walk. One husband, six children, twelve granddaughters, three grandsons (and one on the way) have filled my home and heart with joy, tears and a lot of rooms to clean up! I have been loved, challenged and taught a lot about life. I pray there will be many more years of walking this road together."

About the Author

Patricia Brinkman, after raising her children, started college at the age of 54 as a first year student. She received her BA in Theology from St. Thomas University and an MS in Psychology from Baptist University in Houston. She worked as a counselor in the Texas House, a halfway house for parolees, and was the Director of Women's Services at the Fort Bend Regional Council on Alcoholism and Drug Abuse. She also counseled at the Veteran's Administration Hospital and several high schools in the Spring Branch Independent School District. During this time she became certified in the State of Texas for drug, alcohol and compulsive gambling, receiving the certificates of CADAC, LCDC and CCGC. While preparing for her orals in psychology, Patricia was stricken with Acute Leukemia. She finished her orals in the hospital while under chemical therapy. She has since received her most precious certification, a complete healing from the Lord Jesus.

To order more copies of Patricia Brinkman's book

A Journey in Psalms

copy this order form and mail to:

BROCKTON PUBLISHING
8326 Southwest Freeway
Houston, Texas 77074
or call 1-800-968-7065

Please send me _____ books.

$15.95 per book .... $ _____

Shipping (USA) / Handling ($4 + .50 each book)(tax incl.) $ _____

Total cost .... $ _____

Send books to:

Name _____

Company Name _____

Mailing Address _____

_____

City _____

State, Zip _____